On Stage in the Classroom

Performance Art from K thru 8

Gloria Unti
with
David Sarvis

in collaboration with
Gary Draper

A San Francisco Performing Arts Workshop Book
Second Edition

Contents

Preface

Arts education today has become an entrenched academic field. Currently there is a flourishing movement to integrate arts training systematically into the elementary school curriculum. Realistically or not, the prevailing thrust is to place this project in the hands of the classroom teacher. The teacher will need help.

On Stage in the Classroom relates to that need. It should be in the hands of every matriculating education major and that vast majority of performing arts majors who will become teachers.

It's first premise is that there is a problem-solving formula that can be taught vividly thru the performance art-making process.

The second premise is that performance art-making, especially for those with special needs, can be an enticing alternative way of learning and communicating. It relates to the language arts and lends itself to linkage with the school curriculum.

The third is that performance art-making in a healthy socializing context enhances the child's self-image and promotes interpersonal skills.

In short, cognitive growth, personality growth and aesthetic development are the aims of *On Stage in the Classroom.*

Standard and current works on dance and drama for children teach elementary techniques and endeavor (as this book does) to stimulate imagination. They do not, however, take learning-how-to-think as the central organizing principle. Nor do they merge dance and drama into a single field — a holistic approach to personal expressive communication. This book does just that.

The book's author, Gloria Unti — dancer, choreographer, teacher — in 1965 founded the Performing Arts Workshop (PAW) initially as an inner city neighborhood arts program. By 1975 PAW had begun work in the public schools and in the ensuing years Unti and her staff artists developed and refined the methodology described in this volume.

For her work in arts education in a school population of wide ethnic, linguistic and social diversity, Unti has won national recognition and numerous professional and civic awards, most notably from the California Dance Educators Association and the San Francisco Arts Commission.

The undersigned, her associate author, holds a Yale MFA in drama, has taught at the University of New Mexico, directed plays in Los Angeles and San Francisco and has been associated with Unti since PAW's inception.

Gary Draper (who collaborated on this second edition) is PAW's Co-director. He studied dramaturgy, acting and mime in San Francisco and Paris and is PAW's premier tutor of young artists and of classroom teachers. Together with Unti, he is in demand in California for teacher-training workshops.

David Sarvis
Vice President
San Francisco Performing Arts Workshop

Acknowledgments

Nothing is achieved solely by a single mind and even a modest teaching manual like this reflects abundant input from colleagues, teachers, students and friends. In this small space I can mention but a few, hoping that the rest, knowing me, know how grateful I am for all they've given.

On Stage in the Classroom is the fruit of the fourteen years in which artists of the San Francisco Performing Arts Workshop have been teaching in the Bay Area's schools. Senior among them are PAW's Artistic Co-director Gary Draper and Master Artist Nancy Wang, who invented much that's in this manual.

Gary contributed Chapter 7 and the first segment of Chapter 8 almost verbatim; he was the father of the fables in Chapter 8 and Appendix D. But above all, he tested, refined or revised class plans and elements of the Class Work Bank. He became, in fact, an indispensable collaborator in this new edition of *On Stage in the Classroom*.

One of the earliest pioneers of PAW's Artists-in-Schools program was Diane David, student, teacher and now an officer of PAW's Board. Her support has been immeasurable.

To Dr. William Fowler, author of *Potentials of Childhood*, I'm indebted for his belief in this book and for the child development concepts summarized in Appendix F.

My thanks, too, to Beatrice Krivetsky, elementary school resource teacher, energetic and creative spirit, contributor to this book. Through her mediation PAW/AiS gained invaluable experience over the years with English as a Second Language students.

Finally, a salute to Carla Sarvis, Performing Arts Workshop Administrative Director, whose administrative skills, commitment to our methodology and support of the *On Stage in the Classroom* project could never be excelled.

Manuscript development was made possible by grants from the Columbia Foundation and the Zellerback Foundation, and by donated labor from Janet Pickel's *Business Works*.

Friends of children, all.

Introduction

This little book deals in the domain of those arts in which creative achievement can commence without prior practice and with no other instrument than one's body. It focuses on the age bracket three to fourteen.

The underlying motif is the emphasis on arousing in the child belief in itself, its own creative energy, the validity of its insights and its communications to an audience.

The underlying aim is cognitive development and personality growth.

We will draw from dance and mime and drama — let's call them, collectively, performance art. Performance art is in itself a great classroom. It is a fun-filled way to present an unending variety of problems — problems to be solved, moreover, in a highly stimulating interactive environment.

We will not concern ourselves with the spontaneous, unselfconscious creations of early childhood, interesting though they are. Purposeful creativity involves know-how, and while happy accidents may be used to advantage, the teaching task is to give children the gift of method — how to turn on the creative faucet, where to direct the stream of consciousness.

The method, put with bare simplicity, is this:

- a) Define an objective.
- b) Visualize alternative ways of achieving it (drawing on imagination, intuition, recall or research). This is the key.
- c) Select the way most appropriate or appealing.
- d) Do it ... and adjust it if necessary.

This commonplace strategy is useful everywhere in life — that's exactly why it's central to our work. In art-making the openness of the field and the intense cultivation of imagination make it exciting and easy for children to absorb this creative process. They get the experience in depth; it becomes internalized, part of living. This is cognitive development.

The art-making model has other contributions to make. It provides ways of defining reality which are different from the scholastic organization of knowledge. Art-making has a limitless field of content. It is the most flexible of all the disciplines. It's the best match to the individual psyche. It stretches the range of observation/thinking/feeling. It calls for the invention of new elements and symbols or new combinations of the old. It enhances the child's capacity for concentration, energy control and expressiveness. At its best, art communicates things beyond the reach of words. Such is our frame of reference.

The broad aim of developing the child's creative faculties resolves into five specific goals:

1. To cultivate the child's kinesthesia — the muscle sense and awareness of energy flow through the body and limbs;

2. To develop and exercise each child's creative imagination by problem-solving exercises — exercises in which the child must make its own selections and devise its own solutions;

3. To aim for artistic accomplishment — vision, control and expressiveness. Only if artistic standards are fairly high will significant growth take place; only then will the effort be taken seriously by the children.

4. To sharpen observation, teach analysis and encourage related verbal skills. This is a function of the Theatre mode (Chap. 3) in which the child becomes audience and critic.

5. A fifth goal, of a different sort, is socialization. This will not require much effort on your part because it's inherent in all serious collective art activity and implicit in the class structures described later in this book.

The book itself is a classroom manual, a practical workbook. It contains five short chapters of instruction, four model class plans, three kinds of model performance projects developed step by step, a bank of 150 classroom exercises with a guide to matching them to childrens' age levels, and several useful appendices (including a catalogue of recommended music).

It will serve you well.

PART 1

Teaching

Chapter One

The Children and You

YOU

You who are about to teach, civilization salutes you!

Perhaps you're not a professional actor, dancer or a mime, but you should, at the very least, have had direct art-making experience in these fields. Knowing your material, you will have the tools to invent a composition, a situation, an episode, a scene, and then to isolate and teach its elements. And no matter what this book may teach you about devices to evoke creativity in children, in the end it will be your own intuition, your own resources that will inspire your students and bring dynamic energy into your classroom.

You appreciate and enjoy children's humor. You respect the young, who must cope with constant changes in themselves and with changing perceptions of the world around them. Empathy, in fact, is a must; it gives you the courage to lead the child into far reaches of exploration.

Your commitment to the form and content of what you are doing in the classroom will be contagious. The children will sense it; they will trust you and feel able to commit themselves, to take creative risks.

Your curiosity about life and all the dimensions and textures of the human condition, especially as reflected in your young charges, will surely lead to classroom inventions above and beyond those described in later pages of this book.

THE CHILDREN

If you're a classroom teacher you already know most of what follows.

If you're an artist about to plunge bravely into teaching you'll want a few hints about your young partners in the adventure.

1.   **In the beginning is the body. And the body will be the first subject of our teaching.** It is the most constant thing in the child's environment and consciousness. Nothing is more natural than moving the body, and the body's natural movements and sensory apparatus are the basis of the child's creative experience, its learning. It is the medium through which the child encounters the world.

2.   **Children learn by moving and they are explorers by nature.** The more experiments they do, the more stimuli they receive, the more rapid is their cognitive growth — the faster they discover their own capabilities and limitations and how things and relationships work. Your function as a teacher is to provide the experiments and the stimuli. This book's function is to show you how to do that.

3.   **Children are stimulated by the unexpected, the incongruous.** It excites and provokes investigation. Avoid the predictable, the routine. But use the bizarre with discretion; that which is totally without reference points in the child's experience may create anxiety and become a source of impotence.*

4.   **Learning flowers fastest in a warm supportive atmosphere with expectations of success.** In teaching the creative process, the emphasis is on each child's progress *along its own track*, with a wide range of options in solving a given problem. Any suggestion of competition or ranking is to be avoided. The class should become a collective, with each interested in the other's performance and each child in its own way a winner.

---

* The foregoing three paragraphs are expanded in Appendix F, *The Mechanics of Learning.*

5. **The child's introductory experiences.** We will approach art-making through creative movement, in which our aim is to select, extend, vary and modulate everyday movements and develop them thru the use of imagery ... and later, to set them in a sequence and to give that sequence a structure, a form of some kind, and link them to language. As the child takes its first steps in this process, it also begins to observe what's happening inwardly. This self-observation is important and immediately rewarding. This is exactly how motor control is enhanced and physical expressivity is developed.

Like everyone else, children have different levels of understanding. Some need lots of input while others are adequately stimulated with less information. **But all children will go farther, faster, in their creative endeavors if they are given a structure to work in and specific information to work with.**

Finally, dramatic, exciting child development will happen only to the degree that you, the practitioner, find or make yourself stimulated, motivated, turned-on.

Chapter Two

On Stimulating Creativity

This chapter deals with problems using recall and imagination for their solutions. It has little bearing on the many exercises aimed at developing the child's physical proficiency ... but it's the most important chapter in the book.

LIMITS AND CONSTRAINTS

Creativity flourishes best within constraints and limits.

Children need defined goals and ways to handle the creative problems they encounter. Offering a wide open field of choices often overwhelms and inhibits them. They avoid problem-solving, and instead try to get a clue from the teacher, a hint of what's wanted. Therefore:

State the area of exploration, specify the purpose of the problem and *get the focus narrowed down* to a specific limited field.

Our creative problems will fall within two main categories:

　　1.　inanimate objects and their qualities
　　2.　animal or human subjects in action

For inanimate object problems, only one or two specifics are needed: a description of the thing and the operative situation it's in (see Ch. 10, *Class Work Bank,* p. 93, *Animating the Inanimate*).

For the range of interactions found in the animal kingdom, the student needs information that is best outlined under three headings:

OBJECTIVES, OBSTACLES AND GIVENS

All voluntary action takes place within three variables: 1) objectives, 2) obstacles and 3) givens. Givens are the *given conditions* or situation which affects the way in which the objective is pursued. This includes environment, psychological factors and perhaps body conditions. The subject believes the obstacle can be overcome. The givens must be accepted. Example:

> Beetle (the subject or "character") wants to climb up window pane to lay eggs in the shelter under the top frame (objective).
>
> Wind gusts keep knocking it down (obstacle).
>
> Beetle is old and feeble and the glass is slick (givens).
>
> Armed with such information you can imagine an attitude and "play the action."

The concepts of objective, obstacles and givens have importance beyond the classroom. If internalized by the child, they offer an elementary way of analyzing human behavior and planning one's own actions.

As a model for classroom work, they stimulate concentration, evoke imagination and creativity, help define form, tighten structure and add an element of game fun.

JUSTIFYING

The child must also be aware of "justifying" when playing a human or animal "character". Justifying means that the child must imagine why it's doing what it's doing and why it's doing it in the way it has chosen to do it.

For example: The Player is asked to perform an unspecified action in a confined space with both feet padlocked together.

The student must invent a situation that explains the obstacle; then invent an objective and imagine any other relevant givens (such as state of mind). Finally the student must play an action. This is the most advanced kind of justification problem.

Justifying makes up for a scarcity of givens. It places maximum demand on the imagination. In Chapter 9, p 189, under *Objectives and Obstacles*, you will find some mind-stretching exercises in which the only given is the obstacle.

SPECIFICS

Obviously the more specific you are the bigger head start you give the child toward a creative solution. A certain teacher asked her student to "Be a cloud." Of what use is "Be a cloud?" Where does the child begin? For one thing there is a large number of choices and for another, the child is distracted by wondering what it is the teacher has in mind. Help is needed: *specifics.*

> "Let's say you're a little wispy cloud hiding behind a mountain. You're lifted by a breeze and you wrap around the mountain top. You float over to a village nearby and hover like an umbrella to protect it from the sun."

The big vague problem, "Be a cloud," has been broken down into specific manageable elements, little sub-problems: be small, be wispy, do three things in sequence. Each of these elements echoes something in the child's own experience, something to draw on, building blocks of a creative solution (performance). This is *the solvability of the limited problem.*

THE INCOMPLETE SCENE

Here's how another teacher presented a creative exercise. The problem was to do a scene on a farm. There was discussion about farms and farm animals, and the children selected the characters for their scene: the farmer, a pig, a rooster, a chicken, a snake.

9

With no more than this the students began their scene. They postured and posed, moving randomly with no awareness of each other, no objectives — a confusion of cartoon animals, a non-scene with nowhere to go. What went wrong?

The teacher had failed to be specific:

> *Where* on the farm? Barnyard.
>
> *Time of day:* afternoon, quiet and hot.
>
> *Objectives:* what is each character trying to do or get?
>
> *Scenario:* what is the sequence of events, unfolding through Beginning, Middle and End?

For a full development of this scene see p 247, Appendix D.

SIX STEPS IN TEACHING CREATIVITY

Animals, which have such charm for children and whose physicality is so expressive and so varied in kind, provide a favorite series of problems. Some teachers, however, do no better with animals than with clouds. One teacher asked her children to "be a snake." The children did the obvious: lay on their bellies and wriggled. There was clearly no creativity involved, merely a formless stereotype.

The teacher then, quite rightly, tried to stimulate her students with more information. She discussed different kinds of snakes — rattlers, cobras, garter snakes, pythons. Once again she offered the problem: "Be a snake." Once again they lay down and squirmed on their bellies.

What was wrong? The teacher hadn't given the children information about the *behavior* of the snake, of an individual specific snake in a specific place in a specific condition. "The snake is hanging from a low tree branch, hungry, waiting for a victim. A little bird flies in and perches on a twig just above. Carefully, smoothly the snake curls its body back up to prepare for an attack.

Just when it's ready to strike, the bird flies off. The snake drops back down to wait."

Step 1.   So "Be a cloud" or "Be a snake" is not bad if it's Step 1 in a creativity training procedure, followed by the ensuing steps:

Step 2.   Verbalize. Talk about the quality of the animal's movement. Use words like "lumbering, slinky, sleazy and lithe, vibrating and darting."

Step 3.   Assign a body part whose motion typifies the animal, a part that expresses the whole or serves as a metaphor for the creature. "Be the ear of an elephant," or the trunk, tusks, foot. "Feel like part of that huge elephant body when you move." If the child is quite creative it will mentally add a fly or wasp to motivate an ear motion, but if help is needed, the teacher should give such details.

Step 4.   Think of the environment, a major given. It will affect movement. Is it day? night? dusty? windy? raining? steep? dense foliage? stony? etc.

Step 5.   Give the animal an objective: to hunt, catch, eat, hide, rest, preen — and an obstacle to hamper the pursuit of that objective (usually something in the environment — or danger of attack, sometimes a physical disability, an injury, etc.).

Step 6.   Devise a scenario with a begining, middle and end (begining in the 3rd grade this can be linked to curriculum instruction in writing).

(Such problems should be done in the Theatre mode (p. 16). It's a way of teaching the children how to seek specifics when they tackle a problem. Half the class are Watchers. They observe the entire sequence described above, analyze it and discover for themselves the power of the particular.).

To sum up: express the general through the particular. Basic qualities or essences are best suggested by specific, purposeful *actions*. The child's creative task, given the parameters of objective, obstacle(s) and givens, is to invent those actions.

Once students have grasped the idea of seeking particulars, they can advance to problems which demand more independent creativity — problems of this sort, for example:

"Be two different kinds of animals and take actions which will give the feeling of their body weights." A constraint: they must be two heavy animals, rather than an elephant versus a chipmunk. This stricture makes cartooning hard. To make the distinction between a bear and a gorilla, a moose and a rhinoceros, it is necessary to be specific and precise — and to invent an actual situation for each beast.

STRUCTURE (COMPOSITION)

If specifics give a child its access to the act of creation, it will be structure, that is to say composition, which will make those acts coherent and intelligible, making them into interesting communication.

The simplest, most basic form of composition is the *Beginning, Middle* and *End* model (henceforth to be abbreviated: *B-M-E*). With the foregoing "little cloud" exercise as a beginning, we might continue the scenario:

"Now comes a whirlwind and spins the little cloud around and around, pushing it into different shapes, back and forth and away from the village. The little cloud is whirled like a tornado and lifted high up. Then the wind dies down and the little cloud descends and rains on the hot dusty village ...." this being the *middle*.

And the *end:* "Then the little wispy cloud floats back around the mountain and rests there where it began."

This is the **A B A** form, ending where it began, the simplest compositional pattern and the most serviceable for the younger children. (See *Glossary*, ABA, for other forms).

12

CREATIVITY AND YOU

Teachers basically must draw from themselves. It's *your* creativity, the specifics and the imagery *you* dream up that evokes creativity from the children. Appendix E has some thoughts about imagination that you may find refreshing. It's a capability that thrives on exercise.

Chapter Three

Getting Started

Spaces and Space

Throughout the exercises and problems in this book you will encounter the terms **Home Space, Dance Space**, and **Theatre Mode**, with its **Stage** and **Audience**.

All the exercises in the manual are specifically located in one of these spaces. Although they do represent a sort of classroom geography, the spaces are elastic. They are primarily significant as *functional* concepts; they are ideas as much as they are floor plans.

Home Space and **Dance Space** are most important with tiny tots. As the children grow older those terms evolve into the **Audience** and the **Theatre Space** (or **Stage**) of an imaginary **Theatre.**

HOME SPACE

Home Space (or "Home Corner" if you like) is the class assembly area where you will be learning the children's names through name games at the beginning of each class.

It creates a small, intimate environment which feels secure and comforts the child; quiet things happen here.

In it, the attention of children and teacher becomes concentrated, since everyone is close together.

It is a place for communication, exchange of ideas. It can also be used for small isolation exercises.

It is a quiet-down zone after big energy bursts in the **Dance Space** — a way to change the pace and kind of class activity.

Home Space is where the children are introduced to equipment and properties — drum, tape recorder, etc.

DANCE SPACE

The companion concept to **Home Space** is **Dance Space**. This is where gross motor, high energy activity takes place.. Here, for the most part, each child is involved in its own creative statement, aware of the others only in terms of space and traffic patterns, altho a few exercises do call for interrelating.

The **Dance Space** is treated with friendly consideration, beginning, for the youngest children, with a ritual of greeting the room at the start of the class (see *Model Class Plan 1, Problem 2*). These greetings start the process of learning respect for the place where they make beautiful shapes and movements. Later, in the **Theatre Mode**, the **Dance Space** will become the **Stage**.

THEATRE

When we come to creative problems that involve both Players and Watchers, we will use the word **Theatre**. The **Dance Space** now becomes the **Stage**, the **Home Space** is now the **Audience**. As Players on stage, students experience the subjective process of art-making. As Watchers, in the audience, they learn to objectify, analyze, praise and encourage.

A note about **Theatre:** don't as a rule put the whole class on stage. Use the Stage mainly for smaller groups. There must be an Audience — that's the reason for the Theatre mode. The Watchers talk about what's been achieved and what hasn't. *Thus the next group up has a better chance to succeed.* Thus the students gain from each other's creativity.

Just as the room-greeting ritual of the tiny tots lends an aura of special importance to the activities within the room, so the physical demarcation of the **Stage Space** and the special terminology of stage geography give weight to the activities that occur there. Assuming that you don't have an actual stage to work on, you must invent one. Walk along the imagined perimeter of a stage, placing shoes or other objects at the four corners. No one is allowed within these boundaries unless they are entering to perform — this is sacred territory.

Stage Terms

Teach the language and geography of the stage, as shown in Chapter 10, *The Stage, Travel Paths and Floor Patterns,* problem R2, Page 228. See also *Glossary,* "Stage geography."

SUMMARIZING THE SPACES

Home Space: for assembly, physical quiet, intimacy between students and teacher, previews of what's about to happen, concentration, small isolation exercises, quieting after excitement, departures and returns.

Dance Space: the greater part of the room, the area of action, of trials and efforts, chiefly in motor control and traveling movements — usually the whole class but with personal inward concentration.

Stage: for problem-solving — the first step towards communication in an art form. Those on stage are **Players.**

Audience: for observation and analysis, encouragement, applause. Those in the audience are **Watchers.**

Chapter Four

Making Your Class Plan

TAKE THE LONG VIEW

Good teaching practice requires a master plan for your teaching term — your objectives, materials and a loose timetable.

Begin the teaching term with simple problems within the child's capabilities — problems that are fun to solve and that contain the basic elements of dance: the body, energy, space and time. Having performed and been praised on this rudimentary level, the child immediately begins to feel successful.

Although you will do various exercises for specific reasons (motor skills, concentration, rhythm, speech, etc.), the core of your work is always to provide actual experiences in creativity. Plan these experiences in sequences of *related* exercises (You'll find blocks of related problems in Chapter 10). Children will learn better from a variety of problems in a single category than from fewer problems in more categories.

Constantly introduce; constantly try to *develop,* never pushing technical exercises at the cost of creative conceptual problems.

If your term is a semester, work toward capping it off with a demonstration, based on classroom exercises and structured with a good beginning, an interesting progression and a strong ending.

If your term is to be a full school year, try for a modest production of the kind shown in Chapter 7. These class "demo's" and productions, presented to other classes in the school, are an integral element in the learning process — a testing, a confirmation of growth, a miniature graduation exercise. They are also an incentive for serious work during the preceding months.

THE ROUGH OUTLINE

First Block

Assume you're to teach one fifth grade class a week for 30 weeks and your children have no previous experience of this kind. Here's how you might outline your curriculum:

For starters, have a look at Chapter 9, which suggests appropriate subjects for your age group. Note the lead-off line: "Expand on the foregoing ..." which sends you back to subjects introduced initially to younger children but valid for older ones too; most of them are basic. All this offers you quite a menu.

Your first broad objective is to instill certain basic skills, the foremost of which is *focus and concentration.* Get the students comfortable with their bodies. For warm-ups use motor skills problems — especially those dealing with body awareness and energy flow (inward concentration), and focus with (outward concentration). Get involved with body shapes. Do things with rhythm.

Begin quite early to insert creativity problems, such as animating the inanimate and other problems calling on the imagination.

And begin from the outset the practice of brief post-problem discussions. Lay the groundwork for the habit of analysis.

This is the first block of your master plan. Rather than timetable it too rigidly, however, be loose — be ready to respond to the vitality and readiness of your students; move into new subject matter before the old becomes familiar.

The Middle Block

Begin to concentrate on the materials suggested specifically for your age group — in the case of fifth graders, rudiments of drama. If you haven't yet dealt with objectives, obstacles and givens do so now; there are excellent exercises under this heading in Chapter 10. This is the underpinning of most dramatic work.

It is in this middle block that you should begin to think about your year's-end production. Chapters 7 and 8 will give you some ideas of what is possible. As your concept begins to crystallize, design your class problems so that the learning process leads directly up to the final product: the show.

A Midway Example

It occurs to you to do a show around people's reactions to their environments. You hit on the idea of a crowded bus. You don't yet have a scenario, but you do have a stimulating creative challenge. You formulate exercises that ask the students to explore the movement sensations, the bodily constraints, the peculiar feelings that can arise in a confined and crowded space. Have them decide who they are and what their individual objectives are. They are now moving into scene work and characterization; you are moving toward a script.

The Third Block

This period aims at production. Your scenario gels. Classes shift gradually from exercises into rehearsals. Rehearsals themselves become lessons in expressivity. The children begin to sense their power to create; their power to communicate will soon be tested.

BE FLEXIBLE

The master plan doesn't always unfold smoothly. From time to time you may have to revise your objectives in the light of some new factor. Peer group dynamics or socio-cultural factors may lead you to take a new tack. Or maybe the home room teacher proposes taking up some subject linked to the school curriculum (see Appendix C, *Artist-Teacher Partnership*). If you can respond to the subject matter and if it's not past midterm, you'll probably revise your idea for the production scenario.

THE INDIVIDUAL CLASS PLAN

What is your class plan goal? Choose exercises appropriate to your goal; organize them into a beginning-middle-end sequence (see Structure p 12)

Your class plan will include three or four subjects — the kinds of experiences you want to give the children in a given class. Examples: to work on rhythm, movement flow, imagination. Or: to practice travel paths, add speech, learn cueing.

Base your plan on the use of the functional spaces described in Chapter 3. Both space and time use should be designed terms of class dynamics: small group problems as against whole class exercises; high energy locomotion versus inward concentration or focus or fine motor control.

But never give a class that doesn't have one or more creativity problems. Use germinal situations that require realization by the student, such as those to be found in Chapter 10 under *Justifying, Objectives* and *Obstacles*.

INVENT YOUR OWN EXERCISES

If you invent your own situations, devise them for fluctuation among individual, small group or large group formats. For the younger children, plan simple situations, like a hunting animal, or a child entering an imaginary jump-rope swung by two others. If the youngster is to be an inanimate object, be sure to make a selection it can identify with. Foodstuffs are a good example. Any child who's tried to eat spaghetti has vivid feelings about its "quality of movement."

Other examples: a feather floating in the wind ... a rope slithering down off a table ... a sheet flapping in the breeze on a clothesline.

With older ones, find or devise dramatic situations, scenes with conflict, scenes requiring more inventive solutions, perhaps using language and involving the unusual and the unexpected.

CLASS DYNAMICS

Designing the dynamic pattern of your teaching is itself a creative process.

How are you going to use the spaces we described in the last chapter? Without being mechanical about it, try to alternate between smaller and larger (**Home Space** and **Dance Space**). Once past preschool and kindergarten, you'll want increasingly to use the **Theatre Mode**.

We've mentioned changes in group size. Think also of changes of pace. Think of an energy peak; where is the high point of the class you're planning? It will help, too, to think of the classic *BME* structure — a class thus patterned begins to give the children a sense of composition.

High

Quiet

POOR   GOOD   GOOD

Plan, then, for things to be sometimes fast, sometimes slow, sometimes exuberant but then suddenly harnessed and focused. Contrasts are good, but vary the sharp contrasts with modulations and evolutions of energy; don't get into an up-down-up-down pattern.

None of this means that dynamics is the first consideration. Indispensable but secondary.

What always counts most are the problem-solving exercises that evoke imagination and give the children a sense of acquiring an art form, of taking a step toward art-making itself. When you're using Chapter 10, consider dynamics simply as an *aid,* no more, in the selection of specific problems within each category.

MUCH MILEAGE IN A GOOD PLAN

One can work off a good class plan for a long time, deleting, adding, returning to repeat with variations those problems that seem most to stimulate the children. We have said more than once that cognitive activity is promoted by the unexpected, but it isn't necessary to be continuously novel in each session. *Something* different, yes — but children do need repetition to absorb things conceptually and physically. The *sense* of repetition can be avoided by changing the class format. Even the usual warm-up may occasionally be skipped.

ENDING THE CLASS

The ideal way to wrap up each class is with an exercise in which the achievements of the past hour are condensed into an elementary composition. Thus students get both a quick review and a sense of structure.

Alternatively, end with a final upbeat burst of energy, followed by the ritual of a "Thank you" bow to the teacher.

However you do it, the finale of every class should give the children a sense of a ceremony concluded.

ENDING THIS CHAPTER

It's not easy for a teacher with twenty-five to thirty-five children to work in a detailed way — exploring alternatives and fine-tuning. But the clearer you are about your objectives the more intensely you can work — and this excites and challenges the students ... this is what makes for a productive session with good classroom discipline and good group dynamics.

Chapter Five

Alive in the Classroom

DO'S AND DON'TS

Here you are in the classroom with X-number of children and a class plan in hand, ready to teach. Wait a minute.

DO YOU AND YOUR CHILDREN TALK THE SAME LANGUAGE?

One of your first jobs will be to find out who your children are culturally. In teaching children whose ethnic or class background differs from your own, your intuitions won't be quite as reliable as with youngsters whose family culture resembles yours. Their value systems and behavioral models may be different. So you may have to educate yourself; find out what it is that excites and involves them. Problems linked to their interests will stimulate their growth.

PRESENT YOURSELF

Your class plan is probably good. But no matter how well prepared you are, it all has to be transmitted to your young students through *your* persona, *your* style, *your* energy. You have to be all there — totally present. You yourself are part of the message.

VOICE AND LANGUAGE

Your voice in the classroom is a dynamic musical instrument conveying emotional instructions along with literal ones and inducing responsive feelings in your children. The voice can be like mood music, smooth and slow, creating an atmosphere of tranquillity, promoting relaxation and concentration ... or it can pop, staccato with energy. **Don't be inhibited!** Use your full vocal range to arouse, stimulate, evoke the desired movement quality.

The language you use in class, and how you use it, is vital. Find vivid evocative words. Use them to set up situations for the students' own inner discoveries. Suggestive, powerful imagery will arouse the child's imagination, even — perhaps especially — in problems of kinesthesia and motor control. "Can you twist yourself up tight like a wet washcloth and shake yourself out again?"

Imagery is most dynamically expressed by action-words ("twist" and "shake"); these verbs inspire the gross motor actions, but well chosen modifiers or similes ("like a wet washcloth") will project the finer qualities of movement, the coloration, the nuance. *Thinking* the vivid image as you speak will add liveliness to your voice.

Establish a vocabulary of movement and performance terms and teach it to the kids. The *Glossary* contains all you'll need. Use ordinary non-technical words for locomotor and nonlocomotor movements, movement qualities and body levels. Descriptive language should, in the main, include images familiar to the child, but don't hesitate to teach new and vivid words.

CHANNELING ENERGY

Gathering and directing childhood energy is a classroom challenge. Energy exists in two forms: *potential* (waiting to take action) and *kinetic* (the energy of motion). Class work wants both. Gross motor activity releases kinetic energy; the only problem is that occasionally it generates a kind of wild group excitement that gets out of hand. When that happens, cut the problem short and do a low energy breathing exercise.

Concentration is the organizer of *potential* energy. The student is waiting, alert, ready to move on cue (signal or command) - this is the ideal classroom state. At or near the beginning of each class, find a moment to emphasize focus and concentration. You'll find appropriate exercises in Chapter 10, F-series).

SPOTTING CREATIVITY

The thrust of classroom activity is to generate a thrill in exhibiting one's creative effort with commitment and energy. If the child has the energy and commitment, you'll sense a poetic kernel in the action — sometimes transparent and emotionally moving. Catch it. Speak about it; often the child hardly realizes what it has done but, on being told, will begin to discern the "how" of creativity.

The clearer you are about what you want, the more flexibly you can react to these signals of creative potential because whatever comes up can be manipulated toward your objective. Don't get so locked into *your* way to your objective that you can't adjust to something creative happening in front of you. See it, build on it, link it to what you want to achieve ... or change course — flow with the child's feeling and invention. Encourage the students to take creative risks, to trust their intuitive impulses, not to shun the absurd.

Always encourage artistic honesty — selections, movement and voice springing from the child's own authentic feelings, not from imitation.

Develop an eye for the theatrical effect. What this really means is: learn to shut out momentarily the problem specifics and be alert and sensitive enough to be touched by certain theatrical effects. Actively *watch* for them. And watch for the near misses; maybe a minor adjustment is all that's needed — a small change in design or dynamics.

REPETITION AND DRILL

Investigation and discovery contributes more to cognitive development and skill-mastery than drill does. True, once the child has made a discovery or gone beyond previous limits, some practicing will help confirm the new skill or test the new insight. But an option more effective than drill is to apply the new experience immediately to new, more complex problems. Thus it will be found to work *functionally*, in relation to other things.

POSITIVE REINFORCEMENT

Keep the class free, comfortable, individualized. Create a supportive environment so that the students can take risks, can reach out in an atmosphere of creativity. There is no right or wrong, there is just discovery. Experiment with the watcher and being-watched experience. Shy children should first perform in a group — only later, solo.

Each student should always be made aware of its progress.

Creativity is encouraged by evaluating it in terms of what the child has accomplished *for itself*, from its own starting point — not as gauged by expectations nor by comparisons with others.

It's the process that counts.

Even the final "product," a public demonstration or performance, is never a *finished* product and no judgment is to be passed on it except in positive terms; its primary function is to encourage each of its Players.

SPECIAL CASES

Occasionally you will encounter hyperactive little ones, many of them gifted children but with learning disabilities. Creative movement problems have a particular value for such children, but you should consult their regular teachers about their special needs.

SAFETY

You're responsible for the child's physical well-being in the class and, aside from the common-sense measures any adult would use with children, it is important to teach your students how to fall properly — to land on the fatty and well-muscled areas of the body and to protect knee caps, hip bones and elbows.

Bare feet are safer than shod feet. No skids, fewer falls. Older students are sometimes reluctant to undress their feet. Let them keep their shoes on but encourage sneakers.

SELF-TEST

Do you feel you understood what you were teaching?

Did you cluster your problems around specific objectives?

Did you use any problem-solving exercises?

Did you call on fantasy and imagination?

Did you feel the class had good tempo and timing?

Did you use contrast successfully to produce good class dynamics?

Were you able to deviate from your plan in response to an actual situation?

Were you able, at the end of the class, to recap its main elements in the form of a simple B, M & E composition?

PART 2

Models

Four Model Class Plans

CHAPTER CONTENTS

These plans are guides to good class structure and class dynamics. For easy reference in class planning, the problems in this chapter are repeated in the **Class Work Bank** (Chapter 10), and of course problems from your own fertile brain may replace those shown here.

In these class plans, the first indent is for instruction to you, the teacher. The second, with boldface type, is for your instructions to the children. These should be taken merely as a suggested approach; your own words, adapted to the language level of the class, and your own persona will communicate more vividly than anything you may read from these printed pages.

Stage Directions for the teacher are enclosed in brackets. *[Drum]* is for a single drumbeat, usually a cue to begin, to change or to stop. *[Drumming]* is to establish a tempo, rhythm or pulse.

There are redundancies in these plans; some concepts appear more than once as if presented for the first time. This is partly because it is assumed that any given age level might be getting this training for the first time — all new students need exposure to a few basics. In any case, there are redundancies in classroom practice, too — those repetitions that allow the student to build on the previous experience.

Some terms, some images and some examples may not match the ethnic or class background of your students. Being a creative teacher, you will find substitutes and fine-tune your language for best communication.

The number of players sometimes indicated for a given problem may imply 30 to 35 kids in a class. You should have no trouble scaling down to suit.

This material has been developed with no sex differentiation, even in the highly-charged early teens. Getting into sex games is likely to distract from objective oriented problem solving. Almost every action in this book can be done sex-interchangeably.

Equipment. A small hand-held drum or tambourine with soft mallet is the minimum. Music greatly enhances the impact of the class experience for the younger children: for this you'll need tape recorder and, ideally, prerecorded class tapes so that you can move easily from cue to cue without losing class momentum.

Pre-school, Kindergarten

Focus and Concentration

HOME SPACE

Problem 1:
Name Game

Ask the children to remove their shoes and socks and place them to one side, out of the way. Choose a corner for **HOME SPACE**, and if this is a first class, explain the **HOME SPACE** and the **DANCE SPACE**.

Have the class sit in a circle to begin the Name Game. Softly, all chant, "My name is..." while you point to a child. The child quickly jumps up and says his/her name. Everyone repeats it, clapping once on each syllable. Demonstrate.

DANCE SPACE

Problem 2:
Hello, Room

Walking around the room, the children greet doors and windows. They salute the wall by making an upside-down shape against it. Sitting, they greet the floor by stroking it and bouncing on their bottoms; they promise to keep it clean for dancing. With up-stretched arms they jump hello to the ceiling. This ritual begins to instill respect for their place of dance.

HOME SPACE

Problem 3:
*Shake
Body-Parts*

Call on students to name a body-part then shake it vigorously Move from student to student at a clipped pace and vary the tempo (fast and slow) of the shaking. Periodically have a student freeze its body-part into a shape.

HOME SPACE

Problem 4:
Magic Eye

Each child has its own, very private and personal Magic Eye. It's located in the middle of the chest and it possesses special powers. Inspect each child's Magic Eye and ask its color. Have them shine their Magic Eyes in different parts of the room... and beyond.

DANCE SPACE

[To music] *

Let's take the Magic Eye and whirl it around in the Dance Space. And ... *[drum]* whirl, whirl, whirl, whirl, [ad lib] and ... *[drum]* stop! Don't move! [have them hold for a short count] **Now bend over and hide your Magic Eyes and carry them back to our Home Space.**

HOME SPACE

Problem 5
*Focus and
Concentration*

Place a drum or some object in the center of the circle. Have the children "focus" on the object for several counts. Do it again, only this time have the class watch one student demonstrate a strong focus with eyes glued on the "target". Tell the student to keep its focus on the object and, after the drum, to tell the class what shape and color it is.

To the students:

"Focus" is what the class and (use child's name) **did**

---

* For music suggestions see end of lesson.

when you looked at the drum. And it took "Concentration" to keep our eyes glued on the drum long enough to tell what shape and color it is.

DANCE SPACE

Problem 6:
Run, Freeze,
Focus

We're going to play a game now. When I hit the drum, I want you to stand up and "Focus" on my eyes. See what color they are. When I beat the drum again I want you to run in the DANCE SPACE until I stop drumming and say "Freeze" Let's try that much...

[Drum 1 beat] Focus on my eyes. Ready? Go! *[Drumming]* Run run run run, Freeze. Hold as still as you can. Focus on my eyes ... Run ... Freeze *[repeat until most have the idea]*

DANCE SPACE

Problem 7:
Locomotor
Movements

Introduce Locomotor Movements by pointing out there are many ways to travel through space. Ask them to name a few. *Run. Hop. Skip. Slide. Roll. Gallop. Crawl. Walk.*

To the students:

So, let's review: there's skipping, hopping, jumping, crawling, rolling, galloping, walking and running. Now get ready to run-and-freeze, only this time I'll ask you to travel in different ways.

Have the students run-and freeze, crawl-and-freeze, skip-and-freeze etc. When they freeze call out different objects in the room to focus on.

THEATRE SPACE
6 Players

Problem 8:
Theatre Time

Set-up **THEATRE SPACE** ritual. Describe a theatre. The stage, where people are dancing or acting out stories ... the audience watching them ... the big curtains that open at the beginning and close at the end.

Choose several children to be the curtain. Have them stand in a straight line facing the audience. On the cue *"curtain!"* half turn right and half turn left and march off and sit off R and off L. The "curtain" has opened. Have the Players on stage make a get-ready-to-run-and-freeze shape.

Have the 6 Players re-enact the run--freeze-focus routine with locomotor movements. End their performance with a bow as the audience claps. The "curtain" closes.

Repeat with another 6 Players. Choose another curtain.

DANCE SPACE

Problem 9:
Sleepyhead

To end the class, bring their energy down by having them curl up on the ground and shut their eyes.

> **Now pretend you're asleep. When I come and touch you, open your eyes and don't make a sound. Go tiptoe to where I point...**

Direct them one by one into a circle around the last slumberer. Lead them in a soft chant:

> **"Sleepyhead, Sleepyhead, Wake up, get out of bed!"**

38

around the room, while they mimic every movement Sleepyhead makes... and *[drum]* -

> **Everybody stop. Look at me. In the theatre, when the show is over, the actors all bow when the audience claps, like this...** *[Demonstrate the bow].* **Let's see you do it.** *[action]* **Lovely. Now we're finished 'til next time and I want to thank you for a lovely class... and I'm going to clap for you and do the bow**—*[you do and they do].* **Now let's clap for each other and go to our shoes and socks and put them on.**

Note:

After several classes, some exercises may be performed by half the group at a time, with the other half as watchers. Thus you will introduce the "theatre" concept, with its players and its audience.

Music:
Suggestions:

[a] Bartok *"For Children: Book 1"* side 1, band 4 (first part)

[b] Kabalevsky *24 Preludes,* side 1, cut 2 (*Scherzando*)

[c] Joe Pass & Paulinho da Corta *Tudo Bem,* side 2 *"Que-que-ha"*

[d] Debussy *Children's Corner Suite,* band 8, *"Berceuse des Elephantes"*

1st, 2nd and 3rd grades

Movement Qualities

HOME SPACE

Problem 1:
Fishing
Exercise

This exercise cultivates isolation of foot and stomach movements, hamstring stretches and thigh muscle development.

Students sit in a circle with their feet extended toward the center. Their instructions:

> **Get into your rowboats; we're going fishing. Let's row out to the center of the pond** [*have them reach out over their legs with their arms and pull back for the rowing motion*].

> **Wave and wiggle your feet. They look like little fish — look at them swimming.**

> **Take a fishing pole with both hands and cast the fish line far out into the pond** [*Demonstrate "casting." The center of the circle is the "pond." Their hands are now out beyond their feet*].

> **You caught the fish! Pull it in! ...** [*bringing the feet up to the crotch with knees winged out sideways*]. **Grab it!**

> **Oops! They're slipping away ... they're going to**

swim into the pond again!

Go after them ... [*repeat 3, 4 and 5 a few times and then ...*]

Now let's eat them and see if they can swim around in our tummies [*a quick gulp is all*].

The children undulate their stomach muscles; they show rather than tell you how the fish are swimming within. Go from child to child, commenting on the various ways in which the fish seem to be swimming.

Now give a big burp and your tummy will be flat again.

Problem 2:
Weather Game

To the students:

There's a storm coming. Tap your toes lightly on the floor to make rain. [*action*]

Shoot your arms or legs forward and back to make lightening- "tchew! tchew!" [*action*]

Do rain again... [*action*] **... and bang fast on the floor with your feet to make thunder.**

Repeat rain, lightening and thunder.

Make sunshine. Stretch your legs out and put your arms up like this [*5th position*]**. Turn from side to side to warm your neighbors.**

Move out to the **Dance Space** and repeat the rain, lightening, thunder and sunshine.

DANCE SPACE

Problem 3:
Energy
Qualities

Have the class walk around all in the same direction ... evenly, steadily, not too fast and with no collisions.

> **Energy is what makes you move. Electricity is energy that makes the light shine. Water coming out of the faucet has energy and makes a splash. The wind has energy to push the tree branches around or lift up a kite. And we have energy inside that can flow like the water or the wind to different body parts and make them move. Right now you are moving with energy flowing steadily, evenly down to your legs ... and *[drum]* stop.**

> **Now show me how much energy it takes to ... run! *[drum]* ... walk limping and jerky *[drum]* ... jump up and down. *[drum]***

> **Now everybody stand still ... take a deep breath ... and make a big sneeze — *atchooo! [drum]* And try this: imagine the floor is shaking, hard, making your whole body shake *[drumming]* ... and *stop.* And one more: stand still and relax. Now slowly lift up onto your toes. When I hit the drum, collapse like a sack of sand — but put your foot out so you don't fall. Raise your arms ... higher and your tiptoes ... and *[drum]*. Very good. Let's all sit down and be an audience.**

THEATRE

Problem 4
Five Kinds of
Movement

Class seated.

Discussion:

Did you feel something different in your body every time we did a different kind of movement? Which movement used the most energy? Which one, the least? We have names for those different movements; let's look at them again.

Six Players up.

Sustained Movement

Move any way you want ... twirl, crawl or walk in a new shape ... but think of slow motion.   Move very smoothly and evenly, with no change in energy from start to finish. This is a hard one. Try it.

Demonstrate: *[this needn't be a prolonged movement, but very even]*. Ask the audience to identify who is moving in a slow even way, with no sharp beginning, no breaks in the middle and with no sudden end. Have them bow and return to the audience.

Another 6 Players up.

Percussive Movement

Percussive movement comes in short bursts. The energy pops out or in but you stop it quickly — like when you sneezed. When I hit the drum pretend a baseball hit you in the stomach and freeze! *[drum]*

Discussion: Point out to the audience which of the 6 Players are percussive; which of the 6, if not all, look as if they are being hit by something. Ask the Players...

Did it take more energy to start the movement or to stop it? *[right answer: to stop it]*. **It should feel as if there's something that suddenly blocks the movement, something invisible.**

Six Players up.

Swinging Movement

Swinging movement is a movement that's like a swing at the playground: it goes up, hangs at the top for a tiny second, swoops down and up the other way... like this: *[demonstrate]*. There's a burst of energy on the upswing, then it falls by itself, then another upswing. So the energy comes in waves or pulses. Let's do it.

Players perform. Have a short evaluation with the audience. Ask them...

Did anyone have the same swinging movement as a playground swing? Did anyone hang up too long at the top of the swing? *[to Players]*: Did you find the energy coming in waves, like swinging? Did it feel good in your body?

Thank them and call another 6 Players up..

Vibratory Movement

Now comes the hardest: vibrating. It's a very fast shaking, jittering, and it takes a lot of energy — you have to tighten up to do it. Ready? Go! One leg ... other leg ... arms ... whole body!

Skip and vibrate your ... hips ... back ... head ... whole body...

Lead the audience analysis. Were some vibrating faster than others? Were some more energetic than others? Thank the Players and call up the last group.

Another 6 Players up.

Suspended Movement

Suspended movement is when your body is lifting or reaching out, farther and farther ... until you're

44

almost going to lose balance. The audience thinks you're going to fall — you hang there until you have to twist or dip or drop. Let's try.

Thank the 6 players and have everyone stand up. By now they may have gotten restless, so...

DANCE SPACE

Problem 5:
Run-and-Freeze

Students run-and-freeze with different locomotor movements. Call out energy qualities to add to the movements. If time permits, bring them back to the **Theatre** for one last exercise.

THEATRE

Problem 6:
Improvisation

Two Players up.

> **You're waiting for a bus on a cold, foggy morning and you forgot your jacket. Which of the qualities** *[Vibrating, Swinging, Suspended, Percussive, Sustained]* **goes best with how you might feel?**

Another 2 up.

> **You're on a diving board high up. You're standing on the edge of the board about to take the plunge. Pick your quality and show us.**

Another 2 up.

> **You're roller skating along a sidewalk. Which quality best gives us the feeling of roller skating?**

Another 2 Players up.

You're sneaking up from behind someone to startle him (her) with a hand clap.

After each performance, ask the audience to name the quality that went with the action. Ask them if any different quality might have gone with a particular action. Name them.

DANCE SPACE

Problem 7:
Dance Space,
Ending the
Class

Whole class up.

Students walk randomly in the *Dance Space* avoiding contact. Hit the drum and the students freeze and focus on any object in the room Repeat several times. On the final focus students face you for the bow and clapping.

4th and 5th grades

Objectives and Obstacles

HOME SPACE

Problem 1:
Voice/Body
Warm-up

Whole Class on stage.

Standing in a semi-circle, they focus on you, the teacher. You speak:

> **When I point to you, use your voice to imitate a sound in the city — anything you might hear if you stood still on the sidewalk with your eyes closed. Then follow it with a simple body-movement. When you're finished the rest of us will try and copy you. I'll start.**

Demonstrate, they copy. Point to a student anywhere in the circle. If it is unable to respond quickly, pick another student. It's important you maintain a brisk pace. Keep it flowing from individual to group to individual to group. Don't let your students know whom you'll call next.

Problem 2:
Vocal
Sounds to Movement

Still in the semi-circle, students make vowel and consonant sounds.

To the students:

> **This time we're going to build a sequence. One**

47

of you will make a vocal sound and a movement to go with it. Then we all copy it. Then the 2nd student vocalizes-and-moves, and we copy that and the 1st's. Then the 3rd's, 2nd's and the 1st's ... and so on.

See if your class can build the sequence to 10. Maintain a tight, clipped pace. Don't let the game grind to a halt as someone struggles to come up with a sound.

DANCE SPACE

Problem 3:
Run-and-Freeze Combinations

Whole class. The problem is based on a gross motor action: run or hop or jump or skip (shown below by 3 dots ...) followed by "Freeze" plus an added command, thus:

Run and *[drum]* **freeze! When I hit the drum again, make a shape and freeze** *[loud drumbeat].*

... and freeze! *[drum]* **Make a voice sound with a movement.** *[drumbeat].*

and freeze! Now every time I hit the drum change your shape as fast as you can. *[5 fast drumbeats]*

... and freeze! *[drum]* **Everyone walk until** *[drum]* **freeze! Oops! — You're foot's slipped into a hole. and has gotten stuck.**

Problem 4
Objectives, Obstacles, Givens

You have a problem. You want to get loose. We call that your *Objective.* **that's what you want to do right at this moment. But your toe got jammed under a root. We call that the** *Obstacle* **— something that makes it hard to do what you want.**

48

So what's the situation? Your shoe is loose; (maybe you could slip out of it, then pull free). The dirt is soft (maybe you could scoop away around your heel until you could pull your foot back and slide it up). That loose shoe and that soft dirt are *Givens.* Givens are things in the situation that affect the way you go after your *objective.*

THEATRE

Problem 5:
Objectives,
Obstacles,
Givens
continued

Now let's look at some other situations.

Relocate the class into an AUDIENCE area. One player up.

To the Player:

A hurricane wind is blowing through the doorway.

Objective: you want to shut the door.

Obstacle: power of the wind.

Givens (this is one we just invent for fun): you may push with only three body parts, one at a time.

And make up a sentence or phrase which you'll repeat through the scene. It must be connected with what you're doing.

To end the scene, achieve your objective, then slide exhausted down the doorframe to the floor, and repeat your sentence or phrase one more time.

Discussion: Did the student solve the problem? Did the student forget any part of the problem? Did what the student was saying seem natural at the time?

2nd Player up: repeats the problem.

Discuss and evaluate.

3rd student up.

> **You slipped while hiking and your ankle is caught in a tough, thorny bush jammed between the branches.**
>
> **Objective: you want to get free.**
>
> **Obstacle: sharp thorns. Jerk and you get stabbed. Reach in and you get pricked.**
>
> **Given: you have a pocket knife, not very sharp. You're wearing a belt.**
>
> **Make up a phrase or sentence that fits the context of the scene.**
>
> **Invent an ending.** *[Action]*

Discuss and evaluate.

4th Player up.

> **It's one a.m. and you were supposed to be home at 10 o'clock. If you get caught you're in deep trouble. You've sneaked up onto the back porch.**
>
> **Objective: slip in thru the back window.**
>
> **Obstacle: the window is sticky and jams after you get it started. There are glasses lined up on the**

window sill inside, ready to fall and crash if you bump them.

Given: there are various items on the back porch. Select anything you need.

Make up a phrase or sentence that fits the context of the scene.

Invent an ending. *[Action]*

Discuss and evaluate.

5th Player up.

Same situation, objective and obstacle. Only this time, try different ways of overcoming the obstacle. Make up a new phrase. Invent a different ending. *Action.*

Discuss and evaluate.

THEATRE

Problem 5:
Group
Improvisations

Sub-divide class into groups of 5 to 8.

To the students:

Each group must create a simple situation with an obstacle and givens.

Each of you must decide what character you will be in the scene.

And choose an objective for your character (it might be the same as others).

Use dialogue if you need it.

Now we'll take 4 or 5 minutes to be creative ... and then ... *[Action. Drum]*

Group 1 performs its scene.

Discussion: What was the situation; what was the story? Who were the characters? Did some have strong objectives and some have weaker ones? (not everyone has a strong objective in every situation). Were there any really tough obstacles? Were there characters who didn't seem to have *any* obstacles (not every objective meets an obstacle, but if it doesn't it's not very intresting). Did the scene have a beginning, a middle and an end?

Time permitting, other groups perform their scene each followed by praise and a concise comments suggesting improvements.

DANCE SPACE

Problem 7:
Ending the
Class

Reward their efforts with a high-energy game of Run-and-Freeze. End by sinking to the floor in 10 counts. On 10 they should be lying flat. Give them 10 counts to stand. Then bow: you and they clap.

Model Class Plan 4

6th, 7th and 8th grades

Justifying actions:exercising the imagination

DANCE SPACE

Problem 1:
Warm-up:
Emotive
Action

Conduct this warm-up with maximum voice dynamics, using contrast, anticipation, tension; the object is to *energize* and *feel* the muscles working. The exercise calls for concentration and quick response to cues.

Whole class up. To the students:

Walk to a placement on stage and start there.

Sit. *[drum]* Lie down. *[drum]* Stand! *[drum]* Stre-e-e-etch *[drum]*

Walk to a new position on stage and hold still.

Run-in-place ... faster .. faster ... stop. *[drum]* ... run in slow motion ... stop *[drum]*

Walk to a new spot and hold still.

Now *energy*. Squat—stand—punch—hop—run-in-place ... slow ... slower ... stop *[drum]*

Walk to a new place and hold still.

Jump-in-place. *[drum]* Slow motion collapse. Roll

slowly. Leap up! Stab out with one arm! *[drum]*

THEATRE

Problem 2:   To the students.
About Justifying

> **Movie actors are often told by directors to do various things, like:**
>
> **Walk out of the restaurant ... stop on the fifth step ... look across the street ... turn ... take a step ... turn back to the camera and walk off.**
>
> **If that's all you're told by the director, you have come up with ways to *justify those actions*; you have to imagine *why* you're coming out of a restaurant, *why* you suddenly stop, *why* you look across the street etc.**
>
> **So, let's explore *justification*. Half the class on stage, please.**

THEATRE

Half the class up. Space them a few feet apart.

Call out a series of simple, every day movements to do:

> **Stretch ... twist ... bend ... rise ... turn ... collapse ... roll ... sit ... Good.**
>
> **Now, stand up and stretch to get something off a top shelf ... twist to see who's behind you ... collapse and faint to the floor ... roll and jump up, ready to dodge a ball.**

Beautiful. Now quickly line up to make your bow. And *[to the audience]* **let's give them a hand.** *[lead the applause]*

Repeat with the other half of the class. Call out different movements and different justifications.

Action. Bow and clap. Bring the whole class back to AUDIENCE area.

Now let's see if you can come up with your own justifications.

THEATRE

4 Players up. To 1st Player:

Lie down ... stretch ... twist ... bend ... rise. Now justify the whole sequence *[repeat sequence until student has it]* . **If you get stuck, I'll give you a "why."**

[Justification: getting up in the morning] Player plays the action.

Discussion: Did they see the justification, the "why" of the sequence?

To 2nd Player:

Turn ... fall and flop and sit up and quickly stand.

[Justification: foot slips off the curb] Player plays the action.

Discussion: Were the actions justified? What happened?

To 3rd. Player:

Curl-down-crouch ... straighten up and lean sideway focussing off stage... squat quickly.

[Justification: running and hiding from someone, peeking, hiding] Player plays action.

Discussion.

To 4th Player:

Bounce ... turn ... twist ... bounce ... sink to a high crouch.

[Justification: riding a crowded bus; seat opens up nearby] Player plays the action: to grab a seat.

Discussion.

THEATRE

4 Players up.

Problem 3:
Justifying
Stillness

Use the same set of movements as in Problem 2. But this time insert a pause in the action sequence, a moment of stillness the player must justify. Read the sequence with a pause to each student.

To 1st Player:

Stretch ... twist ... PAUSE ... bend ... rise.

Discussion: Did the pause seem justified? Why? Why not? Did the pause make the action sequence more interesting.

To 2nd Player:

> **Turn ... fall and flop ... PAUSE ... and sit up ... PAUSE ... and stand.**

Discussion: [As above].

To 3rd Player:

> **Curl/crouch ... PAUSE ... straighten up and ... lean ... PAUSE ... squat.**

Discussion: [As above].

To 4th Player:

> **Bounce ... turn ... PAUSE ... twist ... sink.**

Discussion: [As above].

THEATRE

Problem 4:
Restaurant Scene

Divide the class into groups of 5 — 7

> **We're going to do a very short scene with just one character. Each group, nominate a Player (if you have trouble I'll suggest one). Here's the scene: the character...**
>> **walks out of a restaurant**
>>
>> **stops suddenly**
>>
>> **looks across the street**
>>
>> **turns and takes a step**
>>
>> **turns either right or left**
>>
>> **and walks off fast.**

The Player may speak, but the words must be related to the objectives of the actions. There are 6 small actions. I'll repeat them. *Each one has a justification.* Remember them, we'll analyze them in the Discussion. You'll have 10 minutes to work in your groups. Let's begin. *[Groups form to work on Problem 4]*

Let's begin with this group *[pointing].*

Player up. Repeat the list of actions. Allow a minute or two for the Player's mental preparation. Then — *action.*

Applause. *Discussion:*

Who could guess why the character walked out? Why he (she) stopped and locked across the street? And why turn back and then turn and walk off?

After class responces, ask the Player the real story.

Time permitting, run other groups. If time forbids, promise to run any who wishes at the next class.

Problem 5:   To the whole class:

Find a place on stage ... walk toward a target ... freeze .. turn and face the audience ... to my soft drumbeats, call out the numbers from one to ten, starting softly and getting louder and louder.

Repeat several times; after the last time announce.

And now the Bow.

Applaud your students.

Chapter Seven

Moving Toward Production

Term-end demonstrations can come in all shapes and sizes, from simply teaching a class in front of an audience to a fully produced fable such as *The Hunt* (Chapter 8). The demo can be a mere medley of interesting exercises selected for contrast and "build," or (more beneficially) it can be structured around a theme, as in *Creating an Environment*, the process model developed below.

Creating an Environment is a classwork sequence suitable for the 3rd to 6th grades, depending on students' sophistication. The four segments that follow will probably each require the better part of eight classes and can easily be expanded into more by exploring peripheral by-paths or working on technique.

FIRST SEGMENT: SOUND

Step 1

HOME SPACE: Discuss what an environment is; give examples. Get children to name some. Choose one and have children list things found in that environment. Be sure the list includes, besides the apparent things, the invisible ones as well, e.g. wind, smells, sound.

This segment is about the *sounds* of an environment. The life and spirit of the environment will be expressed by what kind of sounds the children select and how they interact and play off each other. Example: an empty seashore. The sounds might be the waves breaking over and sliding up the wet sand; a sea gull squawking; clams opening and closing their shells; seaweed drifting, a distant foghorn, a driftwood log. Driftwood? Suggest that even driftwood, sunlight, rocks and clouds have sound, a sound not heard by humans, perhaps, but a sound just the same.

Step 2

Break-up the class into small groups of 5 to 7. With the aid of the home-room teacher, make sure each group is well mixed; integrate boys and girls; breakup cliques and "in-groups".

Step 3

Explain that each group must decide which of three environments it wishes to be, e.g. a swamp, a desert, a downtown alley (or others you may invent).

Within each group, let each student decide which *one element* or *thing* he or she wishes to be in that environment; e.g. wind, a rock, sunlight, an animal, paper, mud, etc.

At first, exclude human beings from the environments. People and speech may be introduced later in urban environments.

Finally, each student is asked to make-up a *sound* that goes with his or her chosen thing.

Clarify instructions with an example: Group A decides to be a desert. Each member of that group then chooses, alone or with the help of the others, to be *one* (and only one) *thing* found in that environment.

Like what? With the help of the children name off some things found in a desert; tumble weed, sand, lizards, clouds, road runners, side winders, heat waves, etc. Now, each of these things has its sound. "You make up the sound of yours".

Step 4

DANCE SPACE: Scatter the groups about the room, and give them a time limit to accomplish the above — 5 to 10 minutes. Travel from group to group to facilitate the making of group decisions, clear up misunderstandings, untangle instructions, add options.

Step 5

THEATRE:

When time is called, place Group A on stage; have them lie on the floor like the spokes of a wheel, heads toward the hub.

The other groups now become the Watchers. Their turn as Players will come, but just now they are an audience and they are told to keep the following things in mind:

1. Shut your eyes and listen and guess: what *is* the environment?
2. What things in the environment can you name from the sounds you hear?
3. See if the sounds give you the *feeling* of the environment; did they come near making it live?
4. Do you think the group is concentrating on the problem of creating an environment?
5. Try to remember *at least one of the sounds* you hear because at the end of the class we're *all* going to do them. [Teacher: you'll want to note them yourself for use in Step 6].

With the Watchers thus primed, call "Curtain" to begin the action. Let it play out anywhere from 30 to 60 seconds — don't let it go on too long.

Discussion: To encourage dialogue keep the Players on stage, facing the Watchers. You yourself now take on a split focus, treating Watcher and Player with equal importance. Give both ample opportunity to articulate their observations and their thoughts.

Guide the discussion by asking follow-up questions "What environment did you see in your mind?" "What clues gave it away?" "Can you name individual elements you heard in that environment? If no, why not? Did Group 1 work well together? If no, why not? Were the sounds playing off each other like talking and answering? Did Group 1 really give you a feeling of the environment?

Interest in problem-solving will quickly fade if you fail to challenge both watchers and performers. Inspire inquisitiveness early on. Implant the ability to recall accurately, to trace a sequence of actions in any given improvisation. Frequently call on the audience to reconstruct what they think they have just observed; then probe and challenge or expand on those observations.

"Let's try it again; Group 2, up." Remind the Watchers to try to remember the sounds they hear.

Repeat the process until each group has had a turn.

Step 6

THEATRE: In Chapter 4 we recommended ending each class with a sort of reprise or summary of what had just been achieved, preferably in the form of a collective high-energy exercise. Here's how you might wind up this session:

Everyone on stage; you're the audience. As you name the sounds created this day, the original Player utters it again. The sounds will, of course, vary in accent, quality and tempo. Move this fairly fast, but listen for some one sound with good energy, loudness and duration.

Now you yourself make the sound; the class throws it back to you. Repeat it with different tempos and volumes.

The students bow. You applaud them. Dismiss.

POSTSCRIPT

Don't be discouraged by early attempts; sounds will be chaotic, random, inaudible, unrelated to context. Eventually, ideas will sink in; improvisations will become more focused and inventive; the audience will remain engaged.

Be sure to point out moments of stillness and high activity; later you can give this comparison a name: "contrast."

Ask the audience what time of day it is, based on the volume and activity of sounds: ... Morning/wakening ... Midday/active ... Night time/stillness.

Always be alert to point out the more creative, unusual, poetic choices made by some children.

SECOND SEGMENT: MOVEMENT

Step 1

HOME SPACE: The children are told they are going to create an environment using only movement. A brief review on what makes up an environment may be necessary, depending on your class level, their retention, or their familiarity with English.

The rules are the same as in the first class (sub-dividing into groups, selecting one of three environments, and deciding on what *thing* to become). But today the children will create *movement* — the motion of the things they chose to become.

Nothing is totally still. Motion is in everything.

If you're lucky, a student may challenge this notion. Answer by pointing out that although a table or rock appear to have no motion, their molecules are vibrating in a tightly cramped space. "You would need an instrument, like an electron microscope, to see it. So, if you choose to be a table or rock, let us see the movement of your molecules, as if we were looking through an electronic microscope."

Before proceeding, certain demonstrations are necessary to bring into relief the distinction between the common and the unusual — the trite and the creative.

THEATRE: Animals. Several children on stage. Tell them that the name of an animal will be thrown out to them; they are quickly to make the first animal-movement they think of. Toss out the name sharply, as if it were a game of "hot potato" or "think fast."

Repeat with a new group, calling out a different animal, until all have done the exercise.

Unless the children have had prior experience (as in Chapter 2, *Six Steps in Creativity Training*), a pattern will emerge. Ask the children if they can see what it is. It should be obvious: there is little variation in the choice of movements; they seem obvious, ordinary, just what you'd expect.

Next, call one child up and ask it to become the foot of a chicken. Prompting may be necessary: get the child to use its whole body. Say to play it bigger than life, exaggerate: "*Your whole body is the scrawny bony foot of a chicken.*" Be as descriptive and detailed as you can. In most cases the child will be inventive; the movements will become original, unusual and interesting.

Make a guessing game out of it; have children do animal parts as the audience tries to guess what animal is being depicted.

> **Make the point that it is far more interesting to keep your audience searching for clues than it is to state plainly that you're a chicken. Shun the obvious. Discover the unusual.**

Shapes. On stage again, have one child at a time do everyday shapes: those found in playgrounds, on streets, at home. Then have individual students do peculiar, uncommon shapes: those rarely seen. Contrast the usual with the creative by calling up two students again to put the ordinary side by side with the extraordinary (praise both equally, of course; the child doing the ordinary is just demonstrating).

Explain again that such unusual abstract shapes catch our attention because we want to make out what they are — we look for something familiar to tell us what the shape stands for. Such shapes get the clue-seeking audience involved.

Step 2

HOME SPACE: Having grasped these concepts, the children are given the same choice of environments as in the First Segment. They will now select their actions or movements within those environments.

A last word before they begin their creative work: explain that all their improvisations must begin with a tableau. That tableau (and all Beginnings) should *make the audience curious — create a feeling that something interesting is about to happen.*

Step 3

Divide them into new groups, and scatter the groups about the room; set the time limit for decision making and planning of actions at 5 to 10 minutes.

Again, the teacher must visit each group, playing the role of facilitator when needed.

Step 4

When time is called, have Group 1 form its picture. Give them the word, "Curtain", to begin their improvisation.

Step 5

After the improv, have performers face audience to engage in dialogue. Guide the discussion and critique with specific questions: what environment did you see? What clues gave it away? Were the movement selections common or

65

unusual? Be specific; which ones were common or unusual and why? Did the actors come right out and show you what they were or did they keep you guessing? If you were bored, when did it happen? The beginning picture — were you interested or not? If not, why? What did you like about it?

Be critical but supportive. Place the emphasis on *choices made*. Make it a matter of *working* to find the unusual, of not being satisfied with first choices, of taking risks to explore the unknown. If a child makes dull choices, always be sure to find something encouraging: spot some moment when the child approached or *almost* crossed the magic line into the unusual.

Step 6

With group 2, do not accept the beginning picture. Rearrange it into a composition; break it down into its elements, introducing new vocabulary: grouping of shapes (clusters in relation to single shapes), use of space, contrast, levels, and lines of thrust (legs or body lines that suggest movement-about-to-happen).

Constantly use new vocabulary; don't be afraid to ask students to identify some particular element of composition; e.g. if two very different shapes are juxtaposed, what's the word for that?

Always try to time it so that all groups can have their turns.

Again, the class-end energizing group exercise. A specimen: Run-and-freeze-and-make-a-shape ... Touch your left side neighbor's elbow with yours ... Go down to the floor in shapes with elbows still connected ... Stand and release elbows ... run .. stop and turn ... walk forward and make a straight line ... and bow (as you applaud them).

THIRD SEGMENT: THE EVENT

Step 1

HOME SPACE: Introduce new requirements: combine sound and movement and add an event to take place in your environment. Discuss what an event is: reduce it to "a happening of some interest." It can be as simple as wind scattering scraps of paper in a street alley; a boulder suddenly rolling down a hill in a desert; a tiger being stung by a bee in a jungle etc.

Make sure the event has some importance — that is, that it happens for a reason and has some significant effect. Example: a quiet city alley is invaded by gusts of wind causing paper to whirl around, trash cans to topple over, cats to run away in fright, car alarms to go off. Cause and effect should always be there, although causes may be temporarily mysterious.

By now the children know they are working toward "public" performance. Explain that a performance, even a very short one, has a design or structure, a *Beginning,* a *Middle* and an *End.* Our Environment, with its sounds and movements (Segments One and Two) will be the Beginning. The event we're working on today will be the Middle. After the event has happened, the environment will be return to the way it was ... and that will be the End.

Step 2

THEATRE: Using the groups that have been previously established, have them invent and perform their chosen events. Make it clear that an event need not have everyone in the group participating in the action; some may simply continue the sounds and movements of the environment ... the environment is just as important as the event.

Class format and procedure is the same as in the foregoing classes.

Discussion: Ask questions like: Did you see the event? What was it? Did they keep it simple? Did you see more than one event in that improv? How many were there? Was it confusing? Does it seem best to have just one event take place in one environment? Who can describe the cause and the effect of the last event? Did it feel as if there was a Beginning, Middle and End to that scene? etc. etc.

Point out the better-structured improvs — the A B A's.

Step 3

End the class, as before, with a group exercise that pulls the class together with high energy around a given problem.

FOURTH SEGMENT: MUSIC AND MOOD

Step 1

HOME SPACE: The class is divided into new groups. They confer briefly to select their environments (either using earlier choices or new ideas). They choose what they're going to be, how they're going to sound, what they will do.

Step 2

The children now listen to three or four types of music — that is, music which is varied in mood, rhythm and tempo: lively/light/gay .. low/slow/brooding ... vigorous/driving/emphatic ... lonesome (usually a single instrument against a muted background).

Step 3

The groups confer again. They select the music most appropriate to their particular projects (music may have suggested a change in their plans). They decide on an event, its cause and effect (discourage detailed scripting).

Step 4

To the accompaniment of its chosen music, each group performs twice. Treat the second time as the final rehearsal, "setting" the action.

Step 5

Class-end exercise. Emphasize the bow, which they will be making to a real audience soon.

POSTSCRIPT

Such is the process; the product is at hand. Invite an audience: other classes in the school. The younger ones will get very involved. The peers will make for a better post-performance discussion, time permitting.

Chapter Eight

Moving Toward Production 2
More on Process

STAGING POEMS

Three good reasons for staging poems:

1. Just because there's a poem you like.

2. It's relatively simple to do as part of a term-end demo and it has more esthetic value and audience interest than just showing class-work problems.

3. If you're working with ESL (English as a Second Language) children: the combining of words with action helps them absorb meanings. Since they are often shy about speaking out in the foreign tongue, the practice of projecting their voices out to an audience helps make them bolder.

Choosing a Poem

Your school or city librarian can steer you to the children's poems in the poetry section. Too, many "adult" poems whose language is clear and whose meaning is unambiguous will work very well with youngsters seven or eight years old and up.

Two qualities recommend themselves for work with children, whether as Players or Audience. They are humor and conflict. But don't reject an otherwise attractive piece of verse for the apparent want of humor or conflict; you'll see in a moment how they can be inserted.

The first condition is that the poem's imagery catches you, awakens your interest.

Developing Your Staging Concept

For certain simple poems (Japanese haiku or pieces like Emily Dickenson's *A Word*) the plainest staging concept is to choreograph arbitrary movement (shape, gesture, travel and floor patterns) to underscore the individual word or phrase. But from the students' standpoint more is to be learned and fun to be had with a more elaborate creative approach, in which your staging embellishes and comments on the poem, perhaps even mocks it.

Focus in on that imagery that attracted you. Do some free association imaging of your own (look at Appendix A). Think of transformations — how could an image in the poem turn into something else? Think of anomalies, incongruous elements that might be linked to something in the poem. Think of surprises, of contrasts that might be expressed by physical action.

What's the mood of the poem? Do you wish to enhance it or play against it with a subtext — satirizing it, perhaps (children love satire). It is in this process that you can, if you wish, add missing humor, conflict, scariness, physical excitement. It may occur to you to use certain props. Or, coming across an object with an interesting shape or character, you may sense that it can serve on stage,

What you are doing is imagining elements from which to select as you begin to plan your staging.

Manipulating the Text

Don't feel that the poem must be kept intact. It is merely a springboard to a performance that gives your Players creative things to do to earn the interest and applause of their audience. Feel free to add lines for transition or emphasis, to repeat lines or snatches like a refrain, to say lines backward or any other manipulation that works for the effect you want.

The Action Plan

Break the poem into segments (anything from a single word to a short passage) and assign them to different children or groups of children just as a composer assigns parts of his chorale to soloists or the soprano section or, again, the altos, tenors, or basses.

It's best not to blend speech with action; better for the action to be either a prelude or a response to the words.

Write your scenario: what group is doing what, on or after which lines of text. *Think visually*; imagine the stage picture as seen by the audience. Outline the playing area on a sheet of paper and plot your blocking or choreography using pennies or beans to represent Players and their moves. Make a cue sheet with the lines of the poem widely spaced and the stage directions (blocking) entered next to the cue words.

Be sure to update the cue sheet with all the changes and additions made in rehearsal..

STAGING FABLES

Fables: We are using the word to mean extended parables, moral tales told in dramatic form. Language is minimal. Communication is carried chiefly by creative body movement and mime supported and cued by music, sometimes accompanied by narration and sometimes enhanced by masks, props, and selective costume items.

Ideas for fables can come from any angle: legends, natural history, memories, current events, children's stories, sports, poems, relationships in family, school, society at large. Whatever theme is chosen, however, it *must have dramatic content.* It must involve conflict, a clash of objectives. It will need interesting characters and will be helped by an interesting setting, even tho imaginary.

THE HUNT

A Scenario

The animal masks used in this fable can be merely two-dimensional depictions like painted fans, held in one hand in front of the face or when action requires, stuck in the belt. The "fan" should be cut to the outline of the animal's head and painted both sides as a precaution in handling. The hunters guns should be simplified shapes — do not use commercial realistic toy guns.

Characters

Animals in their habitat

A group of sportsmen-hunters

Setting

None is needed. If you have the inclination and the resources, keep it simple, stylized, symbolic. In Scene Two some sort of rack on which the Animal-players hang their masks after Scene One will be useful. They will retrieve them for Scene Four.

Synopsis

Scene One shows the animals converging on their waterhole at daybreak. They drink, play, preen and stretch in a morning-awakening dance.

Scene Two is a hunting lodge. Its walls are hung with trophies. Choreographed pantomime: boasting, taking aim at the trophies (masks), readying for the hunt and setting out.

In *Scene Three* the hunters are on the jungle trail.

In *Scene Four* the fleeing animals set a trap; they lure the hunters into a pool of quicksand where they are helpless.

Scene Five is a debate among the animals. Should they not kill the hunters, just as the hunters intended to kill *them*? In the end it is agreed that only the need for food can justify killing. That's the rule in the jungle.

In *Scene Six* the animals rescue the hunters and they, the hunters, grateful that their lives are spared, convert happily to peaceful coexistence.

A PROCESS MODEL

The following paragraphs show how *The Hunt* scenario can be worked up into a staged production.

The Hunt began with the idea that children are intrigued by exotic settings, perhaps the jungle most of all, with its tigers and panthers, its pythons and anacondas, spectacular birds, monkeys, apes and bizarre vegetation.

But the jungle has become a victim of Man's depredation and many of its species have been brought to near extinction by Man the Hunter.

Here is a clash of objectives: the struggle for survival against the "sport" of the hunt. The theme is potent because of its implications — ecological, psychological and moral (today's aggressor may be tomorrow's victim). But it seizes the imagination of the children because of its exotic animal "characters," especially since animal modeling has been a feature of many of their classroom problems.

The story line couldn't be simpler. Its value will come from developing the action thru a series of class plans rich with creative detail.

Organizing the Work

Assuming that you have your theme, your dramatic conflict and a story idea that expresses it *(The Hunt),* now you are ready to get down to specifics. Prepare six work charts (one or more sheets each):

Who

Where

Action

Music

Props

Class Plans

As work progresses, *Action* and *Music* will merge onto the *Master Cue Chart.*

In the following paragraphs we will use only the first scene as a process example, but the process is the same for all scenes.

1. *Who:* Your story idea already implies certain characters. Now list them specifically, with their individual movement qualities.

    There are two opposed groups: the animals, individualized by species, and the hunters, showing variations of machismo.

    Choose the animals for their variety of movement qualities; don't worry about authenticity of residence — this is an art work, not a science lesson.

    Think of the highly-developed sensory capacities of the animals. What signals of danger do they receive and how do they react? How do they relax, frolic, make love, drink and eat? List as many quality-of-movement characteristics as you can think of.

2. *Where:* The setting(s) or environment you choose will serve three functions:

(a) to establish an ambiance, a mood

(b) to introduce the characters

(c) to influence the action, either aiding or impeding the pursuit of objectives.

In *The Hunt*, a waterhole at the edge of the forest is a good choice for Scene One because all animals come to it; here the audience will meet the whole congregation at once. It is an inherently peaceful scene symbolizing harmonious life. There's a submotif of danger, however: the waterhole can be a mark for predators.

3.   *Action:* Such are your raw materials. Now for the action. What goes on around the waterhole? What will you use to distinguish each species? How will you hint that there's peril in the surrounding jungle? Can you find action-ways to establish that the animals are peaceably co-existing creatures?

4.   *Music:* Since the scene will be primarily structured as dance, look for music. Don't look for something that says "jungle" — seek the feeling of the situation in which the characters find themselves — e.g., the "beautiful day beginning" at the waterhole.

The music will become a flow of cues to the children, so choose something with clearly audible instrumental "voices" and regular rhythm(s). Avoid complex richly-textured orchestrations (see Appendix B: *Music*). You may wish to plan the music as a succession of themes from various sources, entering and fading to correspond with and to cue specific action sequences.

Listen to your music again and again. Learn the musical signposts: emphatic sounds, the beginning of a phrase, the entrance of an instrumental voice, the rests. These will be the Players' cues. Make a chart linking the action to the musical signposts. If you can count the measures, your *Master Cue Chart* will look like the specimen on page 80.

Narration (NARR), if needed, is recorded with the music on the *Master Cue Tape*.

5.   *Props:* When a fable depends on masks or other properties let work on them begin as soon as you know your characters. They take time to make and the children deserve lots of time to practice with them.

6.   *Class Plans:* The fable becomes a frame of reference or point of departure for your class plans. It is in these classes that the children's creativity is explored and developed. It is from their responses that you select what can be used in the action of the fable.

Pull exercises from the *Animal Modeling* segment of Chapter 10. Adapt them for the animals you've selected for *The Hunt,* but be open to other creatures the children may suggest. Using your #1 worksheet, **Who**, discuss qualities of movement and have the children demonstrate.

Run some exercises from Chapter 10, *Cartoons;* model on them to devise variations suitable for the Hunters.

The whole class does all the exercises, at least in the beginning. For purposes of casting hunters and animals, these will be your "auditions." Early in your calendar begin to use the music you've selected and bring the props (the fan-masks and cut-out rifles) into class as soon as they are made. Integrate them into class plan exercises; the children will improvise some fascinating ways to manipulate them.

As you watch the children, your action ideas will gel. Begin to fill your Master Cue Sheet with action cues hooked to the numbered musical beats or other musical signposts, as shown on page 80.

You are now becoming a director. You begin blocking (choreographing, organizing movement patterns). Classes become rehearsals. You think in stage terms — composing stage pictures and, when the blocking is set, establishing tempo, rhythm, accents, energy levels and contrast.

Finally, if you yourself are a highly-trained creative artist (and whether you're doing a fable or performed poems or anything else for an audience) keep the needs of the children and the purpose of our work firmly in mind. Of course your vision of a beautiful, affecting piece will excite and inspire the children — but be on guard lest your own aesthetic priorities relegate some children to uncreative roles and diminish their psychological pay-off. Don't use children as scenery; extend yourself to make them active participants.

THE HUNT   Master Cue Chart - p①

Scene I	music CASANOVA side 1 band 1

MUSIC	Plucked strings ————————————————————→
COUNT	1	2	3	4	2	2	3	4	3	2	3	4	4	2	3	4
NARRA -TION	This is a weird story. You're going to see something amazing!
ACTION	Tableau (establish environment)

MUSIC	Xylophone, main voice ————————————————————→
COUNT	5	2	3	4	6	2	3	4	7	2	3	4	8	2	3	4
NARR.	
ACTION	SQUIRREL moves - goes back to orig. position

MUSIC	Harpsichord ————→ Horn ——→ Xylophone
COUNT	9/1	2	3	4	2	2	3	4	3	2	3	4	5	2	3	4
NARR.	
ACTION	All animals move, change shape — They drink.

80

PART 3

Materials

Chapter Nine

Class Plan Subjects

ARRANGED BY AGE LEVELS
See Chapter 10 for specific problems.

Pre-school and K

Body awareness; the power and beauty of moving; the image of the body as an instrument of expression.

Stationary and locomotor movement.

Body parts and energy flow (kinesthesia).

Evoking creativity through animal modeling.

Concentration (paying attention).

Pre-theatre: body shapes.

Rhythm and music.

Conceptualizing (sharing ideas).

Socialization through rituals.

Grades 1 and 2 *Expand on the foregoing and add:*

Sound — beat and pulse.

Motor skills: movement combinations.

Objective, obstacle and environment.

Animating the inanimate.

Body shapes and levels.

Qualities of movement.

Language skills [for ESL students].

Cueing: word-, sound-, action-cues.

PreTheatre: elements of composition; phrasing.

Observation: critiquing, idea-sharing.

Grades 3 and 4 *Expand on the foregoing and add:*

Body lines, spatial lines, travel lines.

Contrast.

Concentration (focus).

Movement in rhythmic patterns.

Movement phrasing and variations.

Movement composition: beginning, middle and end.

Observation, critiquing, interchange.

Grades 5 and 6 *Expand on the foregoing and add;*

Theatrical movement; pantomime.

Sound and props.

Conceptualizing: describing actions and their justifications.

Adjustments: playing a line in various ways.

Dramatic impact of the spoken word.

Creating theatrical events.

Learning how to listen.

Evaluation, comment, idea-sharing.

Grades 7 and 8 *Continue the above, developing in depth.*

Dramatic structure: drive (objective), conflict (obstacle), resolution and end.

Stage presence and projection.

Vocal expression: timing, accents, stress, tempo, pitch pattern.

Cartooning with face and voice (improv).

Original scenes: with homework or improv.

Variations on story themes and elements.

Observation and debate.

Chapter Ten

Class Work Bank

The 150 exercises in this section are arranged under headings that indicate the *primary* purpose of each. Most of them have secondary values too — sometimes rivalling the listed purpose.

The *Chapter Contents* on the following page shows the classification and the numbering system.

Some of the problems work best in sets that follow a logical teaching progression, although most can also be used alone. Exercises in such sets are headed thus: **Problem X4 (of set X3 — X6)** representing a four-problem set.

There's nothing sacred about the number of Players called for in each exercise. Aside from those which involve the entire class or half the class, most problems can be done with various numbers of Players. Just try to give everyone equal opportunity and try for a mix of group sizes in any one class period.

All of these problems, unlike those in the Model Class Plans (Chap. 6), are written as simple instructions for you, the teacher. You will find your own colorful and evocative language to use in the classroom. The phrase "Drop to the floor" comes to life with "Drop to the floor like a falling leaf," or "... like sack of sand." Specifics. Images. The stuff that summons creativity.

CHAPTER CONTENTS

Animal Modelling

Problem A1 (of Set A1-A3)

FIRST IMPRESSION

DANCE SPACE:
Whole Class

Teacher calls out, **Move like a . . .**

deer	**rabbit**	**monkey**	**giraffe**
frog	**seal**	**horse**	**lion**
cow	**chicken**	**snake**	**squirrel**
turtle	**bird**	**octopus**	**alligator**

Problem A2 (of Set A1-A3)

MOVEMENT QUALITIES

THEATRE:
Whole Class

Teacher discusses qualities of movement, using words like those below (with as many synonyms as possible). The children try to think of animals that match the qualities. I they get stuck, you suggest an appropriate animal.

Qualities	**Appropriate animals**
lumbering	elephant, bear, dinosaur
springy, graceful	deer, cat
wavy, pulsing	octopus, eel
sluggish, crawling	alligator, snail, worm
lithe, slinky	leopard, tiger, all cats
jerky, staccato	scared lizard, squirrel
sliding, smooth	snake

89

darting, vibrating   chipmunk, hummingbird

Half the class up. Each player silently selects an animal and demonstrates its movement quality — all performing at the same time. Audience shouts out the animals they think they see and the classmates who are performing them.

Repeat with the other half of the class.

Problem A3 (of Set A1-A3)

REPRESENTATIVE BODY PARTS

THEATRE:
Solo Players

Ask the children to think of that body part that could stand for the whole animal; for instance the elephant's   ears. Avoid the stereotype, the obvious, e.g. the elephant's trunk The Player's whole body should be used to represent the animal's representive part.

Demonstrate.

The Player performs the problem. The audience guesses what animal, which body part.

Repeat with as many players as you see fit.

Problem A4 (of Set A4-A6)

OBJECTIVES AND OBSTACLES

THEATRE:
Solo Players

Discussion: The *objective* is what the animal is after, or trying to do, at *this moment*. The *obstacle* is something that makes it harder for the animal to do what it's trying to do. For instance:

> **The lioness with a full belly wants to sleep. That's her objective. She flops down in the shade of a big a tree. But a big mean horse fly buzzes around, stinging her. That's the obstacle that keeps her awake.**
>
> **She switches her tail and snaps at the fly. It doesn't help. She lumbers up, moves away, rolls in the dust to squash the fly. Then she stretches and falls asleep.**

One Player performs this scenario.

A second Player invents another example.

Problem A5 (of Set A4-A6)

ENVIRONMENT

THEATRE:
Solo Players

Discussion: Environment is everything around the animal — the space it's in (*small space:* cave, cage, clearing . . . or *open space:* plain, mountain, ridge, watering hole, beach); the things it feels on its skin (hot sun, cold wind, rain, rocky ground, mud, tall grass).

The Player thinks of an animal, selects an objective, imagines an environment, performs. The audience guesses.

Repeat with one or more Players in turn.

Problem A6 (of Set A4-A6)

ENVIRONMENT

THEATRE:
Several Players

The class collectively invents a scenario which the teacher records. Or have each child write its own scenario, then select a few to perform. Animal(s) are chosen, their movement qualities identified, the most expressive body parts selected. An environment is specified.

The scene will be very simple, but it must have a **B M E** (see *Glossary*).

Action. Then *Discussion:* critique.

Repeat with other Players as desired.

Animating The Inanimate

Qualities of Movement ... Pantomime ... Collective Creations

Problem B1 (of Set B1-B2)

IMPERSONATING OBJECTS

THEATRE:
Half Class

A non-discriminating exercise, designed to warm up the class and introduce a new game. Teacher calls out the name of the object; the children "enact" the object and vocalize the appropriate sound.

Old rocking chair	**Clock**
Leaky faucet	**Typewriter**
Coffee percolator	**Swinging door**
Washing machine	**Bouncing ball**
Trombone	**Jump rope**

Other half the class. Substitute other items.

Problem B2 (of Set B1-B2)

IMPERSONATING OBJECTS

THEATRE:
4 Players
at a time

Each Player in turn selects an object and performs it with sound. The audience guesses what it is.

93

Repeat with other quartets.

Problem B3 (of Set B3-B7)

THE 4-PART MACHINE

THEATRE:
4 Players

Players confer, select something that has at least four moving parts.

Each Player undertakes one part, and, taking turns, performs it with vocal sound effects.

The four then "assemble" their parts and perform together. Audience guesses what it is.

Problem B4 (of Set B3-B7)

ACTIVE OBJECTS

THEATRE:
Solo Players

Each Player chooses an object and decides on something that's happening to it - and performs.
Begin with examples (get volunteers):

A coffee pot beginning to boil

Spaghetti — step by step:
dry and stiff
boiling in the pan
soft and drenched with tomato sauce
speared and twirled on a fork

chewed in someone's mouth

A banana:
>   **being plucked off a bunch**
>   **being peeled**
>   **floating in wiggly jello**

etc. to be invented by students. The audience guesses what it is.

Problem B5 (of Set B3-B7)

COMPANION THINGS

THEATRE:
Pairs of Players

Each pair thinks of two objects that normally go together. If a couple gets stuck, offer them something from the following list. Pose or pantomime.

>   **Cup and saucer**
>   **Faucet and hose**
>   **Hammer and nail**
>   **Book shelf and books**
>   **Table and chair**
>   **Paper and pencil**
>   **Floor lamp and light bulb**

Problem B6 (of Set B3-B7)

ROOMS 1

THEATRE:
Half the Class

Teacher calls out the room name and random things in it, one at a time. The whole group "performs" their impressions of each object. This all goes fast, but cut it and send up the other half class when energy drops.

Kitchen	Bedroom	Living Room
fork	bed	sofa
egg beater	pillows	floor lamp
spoon	dresser	coffee table
toaster	long mirror	TV
garbage pail	clock	carpet
stove	closet	picture
cup	rocking chair	bookshelf & books
ironing board	door	record player

Problem B7 (of Set B3-B7)

ROOMS 2

THEATRE:
Groups of
8 Players

Each group selects a room and invests it with props (discussion time will be needed).

The first group "performs" its room, each Player becoming a prop. Visitor from the second group enters the room and "uses" or relates to the "props" according to Visitor's guess as to what they represent.

96

Repeat with next group (the Visitor will now become a Player in *that* room).

Problem B8

THE CONCERT

THEATRE:
6 Players

Five musical instruments and a Conductor. When the Conductor points at a Player, that Player makes the sound of his/her instrument. When the Conductor points but with finger to lips ("Shhh!") the instrument must stop playing.

Encourage the Conductor to establish one-voice, two-voice, three-, four- and five-voice passages during the concert.

Repeat with new Players. This time, if you use the same Conductor, have him/her try for a **B-M-E**.

Conductor uses hand signals to control volume — palm up, lifting for louder; palm down, pressing downward for softer.

Problem B9

HUMAN MACHINES

THEATRE:
Groups of Players

Divide the class into groups of convenient size which will work on the same problem independently and simultaneously.

Each group is to devise an assembly line type of situation in which the movements of human beings have become machine-like. Each group must be specific about *what* the work is and what sound they will vocalize in the routine.

Your drum cue will signal quitting time. The group will disperse, chatting: "5 o'clock" ... "Thought it would never come" ... "Long hard day" ... "See ya tomorrow" ... etc. ad lib. but *still making their movements*.

Second drum cue to freeze. Third drum to cut.

Problem B10

THINGS AS PEOPLE

THEATRE:
4 Players

The Players will select an inanimate object, such as those listed below, and perform its *quality*. This quality becomes a personality trait of a human being, walking across the stage or doing whatever the Player chooses.

> **Objects:**   bouncing ball
> balloon
> dripping water
> bulldozer

Each Player in turn will verbalize the quality of the object, then perform it as a person.

Have the class suggest 4 new objects and 4 new Players. Perform as above.

Nine new Players, trios in turn. Each Player selects an object as above, but this time plays out a mini-scene with dialogue.

Examples:

Three characters are arguing about who does the dishes.

Three characters are entering a crowded bus.

Three characters are meeting to decide whether a teacher should be fired for his/her unpopular views.

Discussion, evaluation, critique.

Body Shapes

Shapes ... Levels ... Line ... Range

Problem C1

GET READY TO DANCE

DANCE SPACE:
Whole Class

Teacher drums, rapid-fire, with a sharp drumbeat for the "freeze" cue.

> **Run and freeze in beautiful, crazy shapes.**
> **Run run run run run run and *freeze!***

Praise the shapes, commenting on the unique qualities of each.

Problem C2 (of Set C2-C6)

LEVELS

DANCE SPACE:
Whole Class

Move around any old way till you hear the drum; then stop and make a shape in a low level. *[action .... drumbeat].*

Now move around in that level *[action]* ... and *[drumbeat]* stop.

Now make a shape in mid-level and *[drumbeat]* move ... and *[drumbeat]* stop.

Now a high level *[drumbeat]* and *[drumbeat]*.

Problem C3 (of Set C2-C6)

LEVELS: HIGH
MIDLEVEL, LOW

DANCE SPACE:
Whole Class

Teacher narrates; children pantomime.

Be a spider crawling on the ground. *[action]* Imagine a rock near you. The spider crawls up on the stone and sits. *[action]* Is the spider higher than before? ... show me . *[action]*

The spider crawls down from the stone and across the ground to the wall *[action]*. It starts to climb up the wall and climbs as high as it can reach and stops. *[action]* Is the spider higher than before?

Now the spider crawls back down and rests on its belly on the ground. *[action]* Is it as low as it can be?

It's very quiet; the spider is very still ... then it jumps up onto its hands and feet and moves around in little circles *[action]*. Is it higher than before? Is it higher than when it was sitting on the stone? Let's call that "midlevel" — right in the middle between low and high.

The spider begins to think it's a butterfly. It reaches up high and flies around the room ... and flies ... and flies ... falls down on the ground to rest.

102

LEVELS

THEATRE:
3 Players (Music)

1st Player is the spider that is very low.

2nd Player is the spider that's midlevel.

3rd Player is the one that is the highest.

They move ad lib.

Discussion. Watchers decide who's on which level.

Problem C4 (of Set C2-C6)

LEVELS

DANCE SPACE:
3 Players

Player 1 is a monkey hanging down from a cloud floating around the sky.

Player 2 is a rabbit deep in a hole, afraid the cloud will split open and let out all the rain.

Player 3 is a donkey who thinks its tail is lost:

> **Look under your belly to find it.**
> **Twist and turn sideways to see it.**
> **Try to stand on your head for a good look.**
> **Sit on your butty-wutt to feel if it's there.**

Discussion: What were the different levels?

Repeat with three others as often as feasible.

Problem C5 (of Set C2-C6)

SHAPES:

DANCE SPACE:
Whole Class

Using voice commands and a drum, lead the children in "run-and-freeze." Each time you call out "freeze" ask your students to make a new and different shape. After awhile ask them to change levels (high, medium, low) with each new shape.

SHAPES:

THEATRE:
Half the Class

Call out different *locomotor movements;* have the students *crawl, skip, gallop, run, jump, hop, slide.* Then have them make a shape and maintain it while traveling in a locomotor movement.

SHAPES:

THEATRE:
6 Players

Again, call out a locomotor movement and have them vary it by:

Making three different shapes while traveling.

Changing levels with each of the three shapes while traveling.

SHAPES:

THEATRE:
Half the Class

Explore making shapes by having the students connect their various body-parts:

> **I want each of you to bring your chins to your knees and hold... the sole of your foot to the top of your head... your nose to your spine... your face to your stomach... elbow to bottom...**

Point out unusual shapes and briefly discuss what makes a particular shape "interesting."

At intervals, have students in audience point out their favorite shapes and ask them to explain why they are interesting.

Problem C6 (of Set C2-C6)

INTERPLAY

THEATRE:
2 Players

Player 1 enters, selects a level and begins to make one shape after another at that level.

Player 2 enters, selects a different level, and changes shape each time Player 1 changes; Player 1 is *cueing* Player 2 (use the word "cue").

At the drumbeat they freeze; then Player 2 takes the lead and 1 follows. Stop with 3 drumbeats.

Repeat with other players. Try with 1 leader and 2 followers, or 1 and 3, etc.

Discussion: Was the stage picture best with just two players? three? More? Did anyone miss a cue? Is there one level that's more interesting than the others?

Problem C7

SHAPES AND VISUALIZING SPACE:

DANCE SPACE:
Half the Class

Empty Spaces. With drum and voice, do run-and-freeze exercise. Have the students hold their shapes. Have two of them discover all the empty spaces between arms and legs and bodies, and between different bodies, by going through the larger spaces or thrusting a limb through the smaller.

Have everyone change to a new shape and send in two different space explorers.

Problem C8

LINES, PLANES, MASSES

HOME SPACE:
Whole Class

Discussion: Lines are one-dimensional. They have length, but practically no width or depth. Naturally no part of your body can really be one-dimensional. But when we speak of line we mean an arm or a leg or an entire body that *suggests* a line — it begins at one place and goes to another. Sometimes we mean just the *edge* of a body shape (like the edge of a shadow).

Planes are two-dimensional, like a sheet of paper and, again, no one's body can actually be two-dimensional. But shapes which look as if the body were pressed between two sheets of glass seem to be in a plane.

Masses are three-dimensional, like the body itself, but the arms and legs must be pulled in against the torso or against each other so that the body is shaped like a mass — a lump, a log, a bag of sawdust.

106

Arrange the class in a circle; you in the center. As you describe the following linear shapes, the students make them.

Vertical line: stand tall with one arm at your side and the other straight up overhead ... kneel with torso straight and both arms pointing at the sky.

Slanting line: stand with body straight but sloping — leaning to your right.

Right angle line: straight legs but bend foward at the hips, keeping your back straight and flat ... keep bending until your torso is parallel to the floor. Now put your arms out over your head.

Another right angle is lying on your back with both legs straight up. Can anyone think of another?

Curved line: turn to your right so that you're right behind your neighbor. Bend your knees and round your torso over. Don't change shape, but turn your head to see the curved shapes on the other side of the circle.

LINES

THEATRE: Whole Class in Twos

Each pair enters, decides which two lines to show, and does body shapes that illustrate them.

Discussion: Was there contrast between the two lines? Name those two lines?

Repeat with the next partners, etc. If, when two thirds of the class has performed, not all four lines have yet appeared, ask in the discussion period which line has been missed.

Discussion: Which two lines seem to have the greatest contrast? Angling and vertical? Angling and curved? Curved and right angle? Who wants to go move a pair of players to show the best contrast? Repeat with another choreographer or two.

Problem C9

FACINGS

THEATRE:
1 Player

The direction a Player is facing, especially in drama, affects the impact of the communication. Player demonstrates on teacher's cue:

> **Full front (face the audience)** — strongest.
>
> **One quarter (face down diagonally)** — next.
>
> **Profile (to the audience)** — weak.
>
> **Three quarters (face up diagonally)** — weakest.
>
> **Straight up (full back to audience)** — strong.

Second Player:

> **Select any full-body movement you wish (for instance: sneak, melt down, explode) and do it in facings, from strongest to weakest.**

Third Player:

Third Player:

Choose a different movement and take it from weakest to strongest.

Fourth Player:

Do a series of movements that begin in a next strongest facing, go through two others and end in the strongest.

Problem C10 (of Set C10-C16)

RANGE AND CONTOUR

THEATRE:
Half the Class

Explain the meaning of range — the span between two extremes. In dance it's used to describe the body's extension outward, its reach in any direction. Let the Players perform:

Push (both hands): short, long, very long pushes.

Strike (one hand): long, medium, short extensions.

Rock (spread-eagle, side to side): short, medium.

Twist (hands behind head): maximum range.

Problem C11 (of Set C10-C16)

RANGE AND CONTOUR

THEATRE:
6 Players

To the students:

> Find a placement on stage. Now make a narrow shape, as if your body is wrapped up into a tight package. But there's a hole in the package near your left shoulder. Send your arm out as far as you can reach ...
>
> And there's a slit at your right thigh. Snake your leg out; send your foot as far away as you can.
>
> Luckily your head is outside the package. Can you lift it any higher toward the ceiling?

Discussion: Did it look as if they really went all the way, the full range? Could you see any extension of the heads?

Repeat with 6 other Players.

Rest of the class on stage.

> Make a low shape. Extend that shape as far as you can. Now try to reach up with an arm or a leg as far as you possibly can — keep the rest of you low.

Problem C12 (of Set C10-C16)

RANGE

THEATRE:

To the students:

Half the Class

> **One foot is glued to the floor. Reach out with some other limb — extend to the widest width and farthest reach.**

Repeat with hand glued to floor; tummy ditto; butt ditto; elbow ditto; back ditto.

Discussion: Did anyone reach so far out that they came unglued from the floor? Were all the extended limbs out straight? ... even the fingers and toes?

Repeat with the other half class.

Problem C13 (of Set C10-C16)

RANGE

THEATRE:
2 Players

To the students:

> **You are glued together at the same place — ankle, hip, elbow, ear — you choose it. You both have to extend as far away from the glued place as you can. When you hear the drumbeat, release and glue to a new place.**

Repeat with other couples.

Discussion: Were they able to stay glued? When arms were glued, did the glued arms reach out too? What else did you notice?

Problem C14 (of Set C10-C16)

RANGE

THEATRE:
Half the Class

To the students:

> **Take a place on stage and start in a closed position; make a tight mass. Now open out into a wide extension ... spread it out further ... and lift, let it grow upward.**

Repeat with other half class.

Discussion.

Problem C15 (of Set C10-C16)

RANGE

THEATRE:
Individuals Players

To the students:

> **Choose a stretching movement and justify it (examples: a bird stretching its wings, a left fielder reaching up for a fly ball).**

Repeat as often as feasible — other extensions, other justifications.

Discussion: Did the movements match the justifications? Which movements looked the most like what they were supposed to be?

This is the opposite: the Player starts with an extended attitude and justifies closing in to a narrow or a lumpy mass . . . the Watchers guess at the justifications.

Problem C16 (of Set C10-C16)

MOTIVATED EXTENSION

THEATRE:
1 Player

To the Player:

> **Your body is resisting a strong force that is closing in on you. Use all your total energy to stop it. (Example: caught in a trash compactor).**

Discussion. Repeat with another Player.

Problem C17 (of Set C17-C18)

TENSION AND RANGE

THEATRE:
10 Players

To the students:

> **Make a circle.**
>
> **Hold hands and keep holding hands.**
>
> **Pull out from the center, spreading the circle to the limit but don't let go.**
>
> **Slowly go down to the floor; don't let go.**
>
> **Up again, keeping maximum stretch in the arms.**

Discussion. Repeat with 10 more Players.

Problem C18 (of Set C17-C18)

TENSION AND RANGE

THEATRE:
5 Pairs

Partners take places on stage, facing each other.

To the students:

> **Hold hands with your right hands and pull away from each other to your fullest extension.**
>
> **Go down to a low level; don't let go.**
>
> **Change hands but never break the connection; always keep a grip with one hand while changing.**
>
> **Change hands again; do it so fast we can hardly see it - but keep that full extension!**

Discussion: Was it really possible to keep a full extension when they changed hands that fast?

Cartoons

These problems are based on the analytic task of selecting certain kinds of movement that will suggest personality traits in the broad unsubtle style of the quick sketch. We will deal with three characteristics: *movement style, tempo* and *rhythm.* They are the *Givens* in each problem. The student supplies the *Objective.*

BRIEFING

DANCE SPACE:
Whole Class

In doing a character sketch one must think of three things besides the character's objective:

> **Movement style — your posture and how you walk and move: straight and proud? Timid and shrunken? easy and relaxed? Swaggering? Beaten down and dragging?**

> **Tempo — does the character think and move quickly, moderately, deliberately or sluggishly?**

> **Rhythm — patterns of speech and behavior mannerisms that keep repeating; they become accents and establish a kind of rhythm. For instance, after every other sentence comes the word "Right?" or after every few words comes a pause. Or frequent nods, quick looks, repeated gestures.**

> **Rhythm can be strong or weak, regular or broken, lilting, syncopated or jerky.**

Problem D1 (of Set D1-D2)

MAKING A CARTOON

THEATRE:
3 Players in turn

First scene: a busy downtown intersection, traffic lights on the blink, traffic tangled up, horns honking.

The character: a cop (female or male) directing traffic.

The Givens:

> **Straight-backed military movement style**
>
> **A slow tempo**
>
> **An irregular rhythm, depending on the   behavior of the motorists**

Discussion: Was the Player able to maintain the assigned bearing? What was the tempo? Did you get a feeling about the rhythm?

Second scene: a kitchen. Player decides on an objective (eg., to dry and put away the dishes in time for the softball game). But in order to concentrate on movement style, tempo, rhythm, a specific series of actions should be defined in advance ... otherwise unintended hesitations will spoil the flow. The class can make suggestions. Before commencing, the Player should recite the sequence of actions.

The Givens:

> **Sunken chest, nervous bird-like movements.**
>
> **Quick tempo, jerky rhythm.**

116

Discussion: (as above). Can anyone more or less imitate the rhythm by clapping?

Third scene: a playground. The *character:* a teenager who hopes to become a pro basketball player. The Player is shooting baskets, dribbling, pivoting, passing and receiving. Mosquitos keep bothering him; he swats them.

The Givens:

Flowing, controlled movement style.

Tempo, moderate

Even rhythm, disturbed by mosquitos.

Discussion: as above. Note that the ball player's objective (to perfect his shooting) encountered an obstacle, very tiny but just enough to spoil his concentration and require a secondary action: swatting mosquitos. Did it spoil his rhythm? or did he use it as a rhythmic accent?

Problem D2 (of Set D1-D2)

MORE CARTOONS

THEATRE:
4 Players in turn

The students are to invent their own characters, objectives and situations and to include a main action and secondary action.

In order to move the problem quickly, have them use models—parent, teacher, classmate, relative, TV or movie character.

Action, followed by *Discussion* focussing on movement style, tempo and rhythm.

Problem D3 (of Set D3-D4)

MAKING A SCENE

THEATRE:
Whole Class

Divide the class into groups of three. Each group is to devise a scene.

Each Player chooses a character and imagines style, tempo and rhythm.

Each trio then selects a situation in which to locate these characters. A brief scenario (1 or 2 minutes) with simple objectives is agreed on.

The performance is improvised. Stress characterization more than situation or "plot."

This may run beyond a single class period.

Discussion focusing on movement style, rhythm and tempo.

Problem D4 (of Set D3-D4)

MAKING A SCENE

HOMEWORK:
Whole Class

To the students:

Write down a situation, either imaginary or something that actually happened. Make a list of

the characters and their typical body movements, mannerisms, tempos and rhythms. Outline the action. Try to use things you've learned in previous classes. You will direct your piece in our next class or the one after. You can use as many people as you need, but keep to a few because it's too complicated to work with a large group.

Composition

Movement Invention ... Phrasing in Time and Space ... Theme and Variations

Composition is one of those inclusive terms which embraces everything from designing a single movement phrase to a complete performance piece. Here you'll be dealing in the first fundamentals.

Problem E1 (of Set E1-E3)

MOVEMENT PHRASES

HOME SPACE:
Whole Class

Speak of how feelings influence the way one does a movement, of how feeling translates into energy output and tempo and range.

> **A movement phrase is a flow of movement that begins, releases energy at varying rates with rises and falls and sometimes pauses — and then comes to an end.**

> **Movement can come from emotions (when you're excited or sad, for instance) but the way you move can also influence your mood.**

> **Most often a movement phrase comes from body-feelings, the sense of energy-flow thru your body parts. Call it an "inner impulse."**

Have the children close their eyes. Announce a body part; the children are to move it at full extension according to the tempo you call out:

Head!   Fast ... slow down ... slow ... slow ... Fast!... Stop and hold.

And then in turn, with the same various changes:

**Leg   Hips   Back   Arms   Elbows
Hands   Fingers   Mouth   Tongue**

Problem E2 (of Set E1-E3)

FEELING FOR A PHRASE

**THEATRE:
One at a Time**

To the students:

> **Use one part of your body and move it in 3 different ways.**
>
> **Put a pause or two into that sequence wherever it feels most natural.**
>
> **Repeat the sequence and continue moving until it feels right to stop .... and ...**
>
> **Stand in stillness for 5 beats.**

Discussion: Did the pauses seem "right?" What effect did they have on the phrase?

> **Repeat the phrase again without the pauses.**

Discussion: Was there much of a difference of feeling without the pauses?

Problem E3 (of Set E1-E3)

FEELING TIME

THEATRE:
Individually

To the students:

> **Select two body parts. Move one until it feels right to stop .... Count 10 beats aloud, then move the second body part .... When you're finished, be still and count again: 10 beats.**
>
> **Combine your two moving body parts, but put at least two quiet moments into your phrase .... End by counting 10 .... Then repeat it.**
>
> **Repeat again but with no pauses; keep moving.**

Discussion: What was different? Which was more interesting with the pauses or without? Why?

Problem E4

PHRASE PLUS ENDING

THEATRE:
3 Players

To 1st Player:

> **Move parts of your body continuously until you feel it's the moment to stop. Freeze and hold. Then do**

a surprise movement you've just invented....and freeze.

2nd Player enters and does a similar sequence, while 1st Player repeats his/her phrase.

3rd Player enters and does a similar sequence, while 1st and 2nd Players repeat their phrases. Cut after 3rd Player freezes.

Discussion: How would you describe the internal timing of each Player? Were you surprised by the "surprise movements?" What did they add?

Problem E5 (of Set E5-E7)

COMPOSITION: COMBINATIONS

THEATRE:
10 Players

A combination is a movement sequence which may or may not be a phrase. It is often, as in this problem, just an arbitrary series of movements without any particular manipulation of time and emphasis.

Call out the following combinations which the Players will perform simultaneously:

Crawl ... roll ... jump up and run—freeze!

Walk 4-legged ... frog leaps ... walk. Stop.

Stagger ... lunge ... stagger ... creep on hands and knees ... Stop.

Creep ... somersault ... jump up ... tiptoe ... run and freeze!

March ... stalk ... dive to floor ... crawl ... Stop.

Discussion after each combination: Did the four movements connect naturally? — was there flow? Did you have any feeling of beginning, middle and end?

Problem E6 (of Set E5-E7)

COMBINATION INTO PHRASE

THEATRE:
Individually

To the student:

> **Do a 4-movement combination — make it up.**

When done:

> **Think of what you just did: where was the high point — the most exciting ? Do the combination again but stress the high point, build the energy there, play with it.**

Discussion: Was there much difference between the first and the second time around? Did it get more interesting? Did it seem like a phrase with feeling?

Repeat with other Players.

Problem E7 (of Set E5-E7)

MUSIC AND PHRASING

THEATRE:
7 Players

Select music that has clear and obvious phrasing; explain the the structure of the phrases, their "profiles" — increases and decreases in musical volume, accelerations and retards, accents if any.

Let the students move freely to the music, improvising combinations.

Repeat with another seven (the second or third seven should begin to anticipate and synchronize with some of the musical progressions).

Problem E8 (of Set E8-E10)

THEME AND VARIATIONS

THEATRE:
3 Players

Explain that the theme is usually stated first (in music, a phrase, sometimes brief, sometimes extended, but rarely very long). Then come variations which keep the essence of the theme but manipulate it in different ways.

To the three together:

Your theme:	**skipping**
Your variations:	**in a crouch**
	erect
	leaning backward
	with torso twist

Let each in turn choose any locomotor movement and invent four variations.

Discussion: What were the themes? Did any of the variations seem unconnected to its theme?

To three more Players:

> **Your theme** *[if it hasn't been done in the preceding set]:* **gallop. I'll give you two variations; then you invent two.** *[Which they should do in turn].*
>
> **... with arms stretched up overhead ... dropping to all fours with your ... weight on your hands but your feet still galloping.**

Discussion: As above.

Problem E9 (of Set E8-E10)

THEME AND VARIATIONS

THEATRE:
2 Players

Each selects a non-locomotor movement and three variations. They begin simultaneously on a drumbeat cue and freeze after finishing their variations.

Discussion: Was there any connection between the Players or was it just two people up there doing their own things? [Show how to connect the two Players by facings, eye contact and "trading" variations].

Again, each Player selects a non-locomotor "theme" movement, but this time *you* will call out, at intervals, two or three single movements which the Players must instantly perform — and continue performing until:

Your *drumbeat* cues them to resume their "theme" movements again.

Discussion: were the Players able to flow in and out of their theme movements as they performed the commands so that it looked composed — not just accidental?

Repeat with new Players, but with a student calling out the interruptions.

Problem E10 (of Set E8-E10)

THEME AND VARIATIONS IN MUSIC

THEATRE:
Class

Select a piece of music with an obvious theme and fairly obvious variations. Play it once. Then repeat, asking for a show of hands when the first variation appears. Play it a third time if necessary, pointing out the entrances of the variations and reappearances of the theme.

6 Players. Improvise to the music, thinking "theme and variations."

Discussion: Did the Players relate to the music? Did they begin their variations when the music did?

Problem E11

COMPOSITION: STRUCTURE

HOME SPACE:
Whole Class

We are dealing here with the simplest of compositional forms, A-B-A — one version of the basic Beginning-Middle-End structure.

A is your theme, usually developed with variations.

B is a contrasting theme with a change of tempo and rhythm and often also with variations.

A returns to your orginal theme.

If your class is advanced you may wish to discuss the classic manipulations of thematic elements in music, ie: inversion, augmentation and repetition, which may suggest certain variations in movement.

A-B-A

THEATRE:
1 Player

Have the Player improvise a simple A-B-A piece as you call out the elements:

A: run, plus variations ...

B: roll, with variations ...

A: run, with a short variation and simple run-theme again.

Discussion: note that the second "A" itself has the A-B-A structure in miniature.

A-B-A

THEATRE:

1st Player performs "A" and freezes when done.

2 Players

2nd Player enters to do "B" and freezes.

1st Player repeats "A" shortened as 2nd Player watches; then both in unison repeat it for a finale.

Discussion: Did the duet at the end do anything for the piece?

Problem E12

Don't attempt this exercise until your class pretty well understands the compositional elements and have worked on them in groups.

A-B-A

THEATRE: Whole Class in Groups of 5

Groups seperately confer to invent compositions in the A-B-A form. Discuss group composition, which gives scope for contrast and stage picture design. Groups perform in turn.

Concentration

Concentration can be classified as 1) Outward Concentration — simple attention or focus, either listening or looking, or 2) Inward Concentration, involving calculation, recall, imagination and kinesthesia. Obviously the former is indispensable to good classroom work; most of the following exercises concern outward concentration. Inward concentration is implicit in all problem-solving creative exercises as well as in body awareness, fine motor control and physical expressiveness.

Problem F1

FOCUS AND CONCENTRATION

HOME SPACE:
Whole Class

Place a drum or some object in the center of the circle. Have the children "focus" on the object for several counts.

Do it again, only this time have the class watch one student demonstrate a strong focus — in which eyes are glued on the "target" (drum) memorizing every detail. Tell the student to keep its focus on the object and tell the class what shape and color it is.

Inform the students:

> **"Focus" is what the class and student did when they looked at the drum. And it took "Concentration" to keep our eyes glued on the drum long enough to see what shape and color it was, to "memorize" it.**

131

Problem F2 (of Set F2-F3)

LISTENING

HOME SPACE:
Whole Class

All sitting cross-legged with eyes closed.

> **Listen to the sounds in the room and listen to the sounds outside. We'll take plenty of time. See how many different sounds you can count.**

After 30 seconds or less, drumbeat to release.

Discussion: Who's got a list of sounds for us? and which way did they come from? Who heard anything else?

Same arrangement. Choose a student to move silently to any wall of the room and start whispering softly. Then motion for silence and wave the whisperer back into the group. Break off with drumbeat.

Discussion: Everybody point to where you think the sound came from. Did anyone hear what he/she was talking about?

LISTENING

THEATRE:
Half the Class

Those on stage stand with eyes closed, grouped and facing the center of the group.

From the *Audience* choose 3 people and, with whispers or written slips, assign each one a specific sound: eg., clap, stamp, bark.

Now have the *Audience* talk, whistle, clap, scrape and stamp, and under the cover of this din disperse the Three to different parts of the room.

On your cue the *Audience* falls silent and the Three take over the noise-making. Give them 8 or 10 beats, then cue them to stop.

Cue the *Audience* to begin again, while the Three sneak back to join them.

Discussion: Ask students from the onstage group to describe what they heard and which direction it came from.

Repeat with other half the class.

Problem F3 (of Set F2-F3)

LISTENING

**THEATRE:
2 Players**

Two Players on stage. Player One's eyes are closed. On your signal the entire Audience begins stamping their feet while Player Two curves silently away from Player One to any new position on stage, freezes there and focuses, concentrating, on Player One.

Stop the *Audience* noise; make the room so still you can hear a speck of dust floating down a beam of light.

Player One tries to sense where Two is; points in the supposed direction. On your drumbeat, One opens eyes.

Discussion: [...if the guess was correct] Was it a sound or mysterious brain-waves or some way of sensing that we don't understand? To One: did you hear anything? breathing? [If guess was way off] What were you thinking about when your eyes were shut?

Problem F4

SURPRISE

DANCE SPACE:
Whole Class

This problem needs quick tempo and drive. You are really trying to stimulate intense concentration and it will be done in part by setting up a rapid rhythm.

> **I'm going to give you a command and then a drumbeat cue to *do* it.**
>
> **If there's no drumbeat, *don't* do it.**
>
> **Whoever moves before the drumbeat is out of the game.**
>
> **Run! [drumbeat] Freeze! [drumbeat]**
>
> **Turn and face the other way and ... *run!* [No drum]**
>
> **Now — ready to really *run?* [Fake a drum stroke, catch another one or two — then drumbeat!]**
>
> **Freeze and touch your neighbor's ankle [drumbeat].**

And so on, ad lib. After this exercise have the class stand still, relax, take a slow deep breath, hold, and exhale slowly.

Problem F5

LISTEN AND LOOK

THEATRE: To the Players:

Half the Class

I'm going to give you three things to do: an action (like 'run') ...and a 'freeze' ...and a 'focus' on something. Like this:

Run! [*drumming* ....and *drumbeat*]—Freeze! and focus on the wall clock. [*Hold for 6 counts. Drumbeat to release*]

Run! [*drum* as above] Freeze and focus on your neighbor's foot.

Jog! [*drum* as above] Freeze and focus on your neighbor's eyebrow.

Jog! [*drum* as above] Freeze and focus on my ear.

Walk toward the audience and me [*drum* as above] Stop and look at what I'm wearing, from head to shoes, and figure out what's new and what's old. [Hold as long as their concentration holds. Then — *drumbeat* to release]

Discussion: Did everyone keep concentration during the focus time? [to Players]

In that last exercise what did you decide? [pointing to your garments one by one] new? or old? What else did you notice?

Praise the concentration of those who picked up on the inconspicuous.

Repeat with the other half the class.

Problem F6

AIMING AT THE TARGET

THEATRE:
9 Players

Line the Players up facing the audience. Tell them just to stand there; that's their only instruction. Don't release them until their discomfort and self-consciousness are obvious.

Choose three targets for the Players to concentrate on — three players per target. Possible concentration-tasks:

Count the seats in the room.

Find the missing minute-mark on the face of the wall clock.

Find the small spot where the paint is peeling off the ceiling.

... or others specific to your room.

Discussion: Was there a difference between their standing there without a focus and when they had something specific to concentrate on? On stage, in rehearsal and in performance — always focus on something specific: object, person, inner image.

Problem F7

FOCUS FACE TO FACE

THEATRE:
6 Players

The Players pair off, then scatter individually to various places on stage.

To the Players:

136

I'll tell you what to do. The drumbeat is your cue to do it.

Run every which way *[drumbeat]* .... **freeze** *[drumbeat]* ... **focus on your partner** *[drumbeat]*.

Walk toward your partner until you are face to face *[drumbeat]*.

Walk away from your partner but keep looking at each other *[drumbeat]*.

Release your focus and walk to some other part of the stage, watching where you walk. When you hear the drum, turn instantly to focus on your partner and freeze .... *[drumbeat]*.

Discussion: Did it seem like there was anything going on between those couples? — as if they were communicating with each other? Did they seem really to concentrate on each other?

Problem F8

SUPER- CONCENTRATION

THEATRE:
2 Players

Player 1 selects an interesting target to focus on while Player 2 stands about 6 feet in front of him or her. Player 2, however, must not block 1's view of the target.

Player 2 now does everything possible except using language to break Player 1's concentration.

Discussion: Did Player 1 seem to have perfect concentration? Did the mouth twitch? [to 1:] Tell us what you noticed about the target you were studying so hard?

Problem F9 (of Set F9-F10)

KEEP COUNT

THEATRE:
3 Players

This is an exercise in inward concentration — locking one's mind onto a track. It's based on 10 even drumbeats. Have each Player repeat his or her instructions to insure perfect understanding. The first time around count the beats aloud.

To Player 1:

> **Do a slow continuous motion for 9 counts. Clap once on 10.** *[Player repeats back]*

To Player 2:

> **Start moving on count 4, fast continuous motion. Freeze on count 8. Clap once on 10.**

To Player 3:

> **Clap on count 3 and 4 and 9. Do a great big movement on count 10.**

Repeat with drumbeats only — no voice.

Discussion: Did that look anything like a dance composition? Keeping the count is essential in certain kinds of group performance — bands, orchestras, modern dance and ballet and some kinds of theatre work.

Repeat with other trios and other count-cues.

Problem F10 (of Set F9-F10)

KEEPING COUNT

THEATRE:
10 Players

Establish an even, leisurely tempo, non-stop for 30 counts. 12 and 20 should be accented; they are cues. There is a final downbeat to finish off.

To the students:

> **The problem is to keep track of the counts while you're improvising movements. Count out loud if you wish.**

> **Drumbeat *one* is your cue to begin doing a slow motion phrase. Freeze on *ten*. Hold for one count, and ...**

> **Start on *twelve* — a six-beat fast action phrase — freeze on *eighteen*. Hold for one count and...**

> **Start on *twenty* — your slow motion phrase again. Freeze on *twenty-nine*. Release on *thirty*.**

Run over it again before starting — a 10-count slow motion phrase, a hold, a 6-count fast motion phrase, a hold, a repeat of the 10-count phrase.

Repeat with another group.

Problem F11 (of Set F11-F13)

FOCUS AND COMPOSITION

THEATRE:
2 Players

The Players must take body shapes that have contrasting levels. During this exercise either one may change level, but the other must then change, if necessary to keep a contrast.

To the students:

> **Focus on each other. Now move a knee toward the other Player. Keep your focus.**
>
> **Now move any other body part toward the other Player.**
>
> **Now change levels and take a long sliding step toward each other. Keep the focus.**
>
> **Reach out one arm to your partner. Change levels and reach out both arms.**
>
> **Stand up straight, facing each other. Keep your focus but turn your bodies full front to the audience.**
>
> **At the drumbeat, look at the audience.** *[drumbeat].*

Discussion: Did this look anything like the beginning of a dance or a scene from a play? Did their concentration make what you saw seem important?

Repeat with the next 3 Players.

Problem F12 (of Set F11-F13)

FOCUS AND SPACE RELATIONSHIPS

THEATRE:
6 Players

Three Players offstage on either side with backs to the audience. If you're not sure of their names, give them numbers.

The following directions are the same for all Players, altho they enter and perform one at a time.

> **Enter on the drumbeat after I call your name *[or number]*. Then I'll give commands, each one followed by a drumbeat cue. Move on cue.**
>
> **When each of you enters the stage space, be aware of design — of how your body attitude and your focus will relate to or contrast with other Players on stage. Ready?**
>
> **Player One, enter *[drumbeat]*. Focus on any target you wish *[drumbeat]*.**
>
> **Walk toward your target *[drumbeat]*. Take a position facing any way you like *[drumbeat]*. Hold focus.**
>
> **Holding your focus, change shape *[drumbeat]*.**
>
> **Choose a new target; walk toward it; stop and make a shape *[drumbeat]*.**
>
> **Change your level in that shape *[drumbeat]*. ... and hold until the last one has finished.**

Now the next Player and the rest in turn.

Discussion: Did it seem as if they didn't know anyone else was there? Did you think that the ones who came on later were finding positions and shapes that worked well with those already on stage? Did the final stage picture look anything like a composition?

Problem 13 (of Set F11-F13)

FOCUS AND SPACE RELATIONSHIPS

THEATRE:
8 PLAYERS

Four pairs in four locations on stage. Partners sit on the floor facing each other.

Close your eyes and be still; be ready for action.

Open your eyes and focus on your partner's mouth.

Let your eyes go past your partner to another Player or object.

Release your focus; still sitting, turn your back on your partner.

Rise and walk away from your partner, focussing on something ahead of you.

Turn and face your partner; focus on your partner's face.

Walk toward each other, keeping focussed.

Stop and focus on another Player — a specific target like hair, chin, neck.

Walk toward that Player.

Freeze and hold focus for 10 drumbeats.

Discussion: See how the feeling changed when the focus shifted to other Players? Did it seem to mean anything? Was there energy and concentration?

Note: The above exercise can be developed into a scene in any one of several locales — any public place.

Problem F14 (of Set F14-F15)

INWARD CONCENTRATION

THEATRE:
6 Players

Have the six face the audience. Demonstrate the "neutral position" — standing with weight balanced evenly on both feet, arms hanging and hands lightly clasped in front.

To the students:

> **Please take the neutral position and close your eyes. When I call your name, move one body part and come back to neutral. Then move a different part ... and come back to neutral. I'll go right down the line ...** *[You do].*

> **Now when I call your name, again choose a body part and move it. Keep it moving as long as you feel it should be moved.**

> **When you bring it to a stop, freeze for a moment ... go to neutral and stay in neutral position until everyone is finished.**

Discussion: Did it seem as if they were feeling some energy moving around in the body part?

Repeat with another sextet.

Problem F15 (of Set F14-F15)

BUZZY BEE

THEATRE:
2 Players

A fantasy/concentration exercise for tinytots:

> **Imagine a bee flying thru a window into the room. Where is it? ...Follow it with your eyes and head. Did it go out the door? Is it on your toe? Watch it fly around in great big circles .... and off it goes thru the window.**

Choose another child who is to imagine another bee and follow it with eyes and head. The bee alights and the child freezes. The class must guess where the bee landed. Repeat with other students.

Cues

Word cues ... Movement cues ... Sound cues

Define "cue." Explain that a cue is any kind of a signal that tells you it's your turn to do something or say something. There are word cues; there are movement cues, which is when someone else makes a movement that sends you a signal; and there are sound cues like the drumbeat we use in class.

Problem G1

WORD CUES 1

THEATRE:
Half the Class

Conduct this warm-up with maximum voice dynamics, using contrast, anticipation, tension; the object is to *energize* and *feel* the muscles working. The exercise calls for concentration and quick response to cues.

To the students:

> **Walk to a placement on stage and stand there.**
>
> **Sit ... lie down ... stand! ... stre-e-e-etch** *[drum].*
>
> **Walk to a new spot on stage and hold still.**
>
> **Run-in-place ... faster ... faster ... stop ... run in slow motion ... stop** *[drum].*
>
> **Walk to a new spot and hold still. Now, *energy!***

Squat-stand-punch-chop-run in place ... slow ... slower ... stop *[drum]*

Walk to a new spot and hold still.

Jump-in-place ... slow motion collapse ... roll slowly ... *leap up!* stab out with one arm! *[drum]*

Problem G2

WORD CUES 2

THEATRE:
Half the Class

To the students:

I'm going to give you an action word, like "hop" or "sit down" or "crawl." Then I'll say a sentence that has that word in it.

When you hear that word, it's your cue to *do* that action. Stop when you hear the drumbeat.

The first word cue is "run." When you hear it, run! Now listen:

"If you see a dinosaur in the grocery store run home and tell your father".

[They are running — give them a few seconds, then drumbeat. If several missed the cue, do a rerun.]

Next: your cue is "skip." Here's the sentence: "When I get to the boring part I always skip it because — well, just because." *[Action ..... drumbeat to stop].*

146

The cue is "crawl." ... "I'd crawl a mile for a chocolate milkshake." *[Action .. drumbeat].*

The cue is "sit down." ... "The poor dog was dog-tired and when dogs like that dog are dog-tired they sit down even in the doggone street. *[Action]* Stay down, because the next cue is:

"Get up." ... "Get up! Time to get dressed." *[and drumbeat].*

Comment (if appropriate) — not everyone picked up really quickly on the cues; it takes good concentration to catch a cue, doesn't it?

Problem G3

WORD CUES 3

THEATRE:
10 Players

Give each Player a number from one to ten. Have them run and freeze. When they are "frozen" call out those numbers in random order. The students respond to their assigned numbers by calling out their names.

Repeat until the whole class has done it.

Repeat but tell the children:

When you hear your number, call out anything that pops into your head — like "grandma" — "stairs" — "green" — "Tommy" — "ice cube" — "stop sign" — "lizard" — "slow" — anything.

Repeat with another ten.

Problem G4

THEATRE:
Whole Class

Divide the class into three groups and have each group count off beginning with "One"so that each player in each group has a number.

> **Remember your numbers! Group One, up. Begin walking around. When your number is called touch someone nearest you. Whomever is touched must call out the name of a food and quickly change direction** [to make it interesting, call numbers out of sequence and varying the tempo of your call. This adds suspense, keeps them off balance].

Call *Freeze [drumbeat];* they hold while...

> **Group Two, go on stage and walk in slow motion. When your number is called touch whomever you pass. If *you* are touched, call out the name of a pop singer and quickly change direction. For those of you *not* touched, keep moving in slow motion.**

Call *Freeze as above;* they hold while...

> **Group Three enters running and dodging. When your number is called touch whomever you pass. If *you* are touched, call out the name of someone in class and quickly change direction. If *you* aren't touched, keep on running and dodging.**

Call *Freeze as above.* Release.

Discussion: was it hard to concentrate on your cues when you were moving? Did you remember what to say when you got your cue?

148

Problem G5

HOME SPACE:
Whole Class

Half the class is *Announcers*, half is *Chorus*.

Teach them following lines. Each line is the other group's cue.

Announcers:	*Chorus:*
I am.	**Whadje say?**
I am what I feel.	**I don't believe it.**
I am what I think.	**Sez who, sez who?**
I am what I do..	**Who d'you think you are?**
I am somebody.	**Well, pleased to meetcha.**

Run them through it. Switch roles and repeat.

Add movements. The cue is now the *end* of the other group's movement. The first time through use your drumbeat to cut off the movement and give a feel for the timing.

I am. *[Hands clasped overhead, maximum range.]*

Whatje say? *[Hands on hips; lean forward.]*

I am what I feel. *[Twirl three times.]*

I don't believe it. *[Clap, turn away.]*

I am what I think. *[2 steps backward, 3 forward.]*

Sez who, sez who? *[Clap, turn back.]*

I am what I do. *[Golf club swing, twice.]*

Who d'you think you are? *[Lunge forward.]*

I am somebody. *[Jump, throwing arms up in a V.]*

Well, pleased to meetcha. *[Shrug, turn away, walk off.]*

Reverse roles and repeat without the drum.

Divide class into groups of 5 to 7. Have them choose a subject or situation, a point of view about it, and their own words and movement.

Justifying

Using the imagination to supply the specifics that have not been given by the teacher, director or script.

Problem H1(of Set H1-H2)

JUSTIFYING

THEATRE:
3 Players in turn

Review **justifying** for the class (See page 54):

> **Justifying is imagining why you're doing what you're doing and why you you're doing it the *way* you're doing it.**

To the Players:

> **I'll give you each an action. Take a minute to think of why you might be doing it. Then do it. If you get stuck ask me for an example, then do that.**

Player 1:

> **Run on a diagonal line but stop abruptly. Justify the action.**

Example: running to catch the bus, you suddenly remember you left your money at home.

Player 2:

Walk in a large circle, looking up.

Studying a great tall statue.

Player 3:

Stroll up and down in a straight line.

On a picket line at a nuclear waste dump.

Discussion: Can anyone imagine any other justifications for those actions? (And if the above examples weren't used:) Did any of you guess what the Players were doing?

JUSTIFYING

THEATRE
4 Players in turn

To the four Players:

I'll call out some common, every day movements and each one of you will do them once, then try to think of a justification before doing them again "for real."

1 st Player up.

Lie down ... stretch ... twist ... bend ... rise. Now justify. If you get stuck, I'll give you a "why."

[Justification: getting up in the morning]. Player does the action.

2 nd Player up.

Turn ... collapse ... sit.

[Justification: foot slips off the curb]. Player does the action.

152

3rd Player up.

> **Curl-down-crouch ... straighten-up ... lean sideways ... squat.**

[Justification: running and hiding from someone, peeking, hiding]. Player plays the action.

4th Player up.

> **Bounce ... turn ... twist ... sink to a high crouch.**

[Justification: riding a crowded bus; seat opens up nearby]. Player plays the action: to grab a seat.

Problem H2 (of Set H1-H2)

JUSTIFYING STILLNESS

THEATRE:
4 Players

Read the set of movements with the *"pause"*, to the students and have them take a moment to justify the pause within a little scenario. Read the set again and, if necessary, prompt the students as they play the action.

To the students:

> **Stretch ... twist ... PAUSE ... bend ... rise.**

> **Turn ... collapse ... PAUSE ... roll ... PAUSE ... sit.**

> **Curl\crouch ... PAUSE ... uncurl ... lean ... PAUSE ... squat.**

> **Bounce ... turn ... PAUSE ... twist ... sink.**

Discussion: Why did the Player pause at that moment? Guess. Was there good concentration? Did the pauses make it more interesting? Could you tell what motivated them?

Problem H3 (of Set H3-H5)

JUSTIFYING PAUSES

THEATRE:
5 Players in turn

Player 1:

> **Pick up the phone; pause halfway; put it down again.**

Discussion: What caused the pause? [To the Player:] So what was it?

To Player 2:

> **You're a ball player up to bat, all set to swing at the next pitch. Suddenly you straighten up and let the bat hang.**

Discussion: Did you get a clue from where the hitter was looking before the pause?

Player 3:

> **You're walking along and suddenly you stop, pause to perform a small quick action, walk on.**

Discussion: What was the small quick action? Was it really necessary to pause to do it?

Player 4:

154

You're on your hands and knees on the rug looking for some tiny thing you've lost. You pause, stare for a long minute, then begin hunting again.

Discussion: Did any Watchers invent justifications *before* the action? During it? After?

Player 5:

You're climbing a ladder. You pause, look up, climb back down again.

Discussion: What do you suppose that ladder climber saw up there?

Problem H4 (of Set H3-H5)

IMAGINATION EVENTS

THEATRE:
1 Player

Give each Player a short combination of movements and have her/him justify it *(by justifying we mean imagining a situation you're in and what it is you're trying to do).*

Player 1 up.

Walk ... stagger ... crawl ... stagger.

If necessary, whisper the situation to the Player: The Player has just drunk a poisoned drink. Call the movements:

Action.

Discussion: Why was the actor acting like that? *[There's more than one valid answer.]* Could you feel the sharp pain in the belly? Did you think there was inward concentration?

Player 2 up. Same agenda. The situation: the kid has just won the lottery. The movements:

Jump ... skip ... twirl ... clap.

Action. *Discussion.*

Problem H5 (of Set H3-H5)

JUSTIFYING

THEATRE:
Several Players
in turn

Divide those who haven't performed into two groups. Players of the first group devise and, in turn, perform their own actions with two pauses each. (Example: walk .. pause .. start to sit .. pause .. sit). Give them a little time to generate their ideas.

Players of the second group watch the first group Players perform and either: (a) think of a third pause to add to the action, or (b) plan some different action with two pauses.

First group performs.

Discussion: as above. Second group may need another minute or two to think before performing.

Players of the second group perform in turn.

Discussion: as above.

Problem H6

There is something on your skin or hair. It can be solid or liquid. It can be alive or dead, animal, vegetable or mineral. It can be moving or motionless.

Invent it. Get it off you.

Discussion: Guessing game — what was it? Did it upset or hurt or bother the Player? Was the right amount of energy used?

Establish something on your body, just like the previous Player did. You want to get rid of it but you can't use your hands.

What is it? Why can't you use your hands? What can you do? Try to do it. Maybe you can, maybe you can't.

Example (you may want to hold this back unless the Player draws a complete blank): A waiter is entering the dining room carrying, with both hands, a big loaded tray of food. There's a cockroach on his neck, traveling toward his face.

Discussion: Did the Player solve the problem? What was the Thing?

Problem H7

THEATRE:
Players singly

Call out the following movement combinations. Before they are performed whisper the justification to the Player. In these problems the Watchers must propose justifications after seeing the action.

Crawl, roll, jump, run.

Justification: escaping from somebody.

Discussion: What was happening? Why those movements? (After responses:) was there good concentration? Energy?

Run, turn a corner, walk slowly, then fast.

Justification: a detective tailing a suspect.

Discussion: as above

On your knees, curl down, hold, straighten up slowly, look upstage, sink down. again. Do it twice.

Justification: hiding from somebody.

Discussion: as above.

Walk, stagger, crawl on hands and knees, rise and stagger.

Justification: .. has just drunk a poisoned drink.

Discussion: as above.

Jump, skip in a circle, hop, jump and clap.

158

Justification: .. has just won the lottery.

Discussion: as above.

Stretch, twist, bend, straighten, shuffle.

Justification: .. has just gotten out of bed.

Problem H8

JUSTIFYING

THEATRE:
2 Players

The students are in the Principal's office, waiting. They don't know why the Principal has called them in. Each Player must keep moving, except for brief pauses. The movements must be justified.

Stop the exercise when it's gone on long enough.

Discussion: Were they scared or just restless or calm? What did you see them doing while they waited?

Problem H9

JUSTIFYING DIALOGUE

THEATRE:
2 Players

Players onstage. Each one has one line to say but speaks twice, using two different justifications. Give the Players their instructions out of earshot of the class.

To Player 1:

Your line is, "I don't feel like going to school today."

Justification: belly ache.

Player 2's answer: "There's a dead body in the basement."

Justification: get help to revive the corpse.

Player 1's response: Same line but different justification:

To suggest that they both sneak off and go downtown.

Player 2's answer Same line but different justification:

To fool his friend into looking in the basement.

Let them do it again, or send up another pair.

Discussion: Guess the justifications. Did the Players have good concentration? Did it seem real or more as if they were sending you a hint?

Problem H10

JUSTIFYING

THEATRE:
6 Players

There is a lifeboat; the ship has gone down. Seat them on chairs or on the floor, roughly in rows but not exactly side by side — don't give the game away by staging. Give the Players the following directions out of earshot of the class.

Close your eyes. Each of you can say just one sentence. Don't speak until you can remember what the ship looked like when one end tipped up and it slowly slipped into the sea. You will feel the ocean all around you stretching as far as you can see. You have never felt so lonely in your life. Don't answer anyone; don't interrupt anyone. Just say your thought when you feel ready.

Go back to the Watchers. Quietly say "Curtain."

Discussion: When did you realize what had happened? Did everyone have good concentration? feeling about the scene? To the Players: probe the "reality" of their feelings: what color was the water? How high the waves? Thoughts about what might happen later ... ?

If the class dynamic feels right let another group do the exercise.

Other group situation problems:

Exploring a cavern with flashlights.

In a classroom with black smoke coming in under the hall door.

Others invented by the class.

In each case, develop the environment with detailed imagery. What is the situation — the givens? Why is the group there; what is the group objective? Are there other individual objectives?

After this preparation give a moment of silence, then the word, "Curtain."

161

Loosening Up

Many children are too inhibited to realize their potential in creative work as performers. The following problems accessing sensations beyond the usual will extend the child's range of expression.

Problem J1

NAME GAME

HOME SPACE:
Whole Class

Ask the children to remove their shoes and socks and place them to one side, out of the way. Choose a corner for HOME SPACE, and if this is a first class, explain the HOME SPACE and the DANCE SPACE.

Have class sit in a circle to begin **Name Game**. All chant, "My name is..." while you point to a child. The child quickly jumps up and says its name. Everyone repeats it, clapping once on each syllable. Demonstrate.

Problem J2

HELLO, ROOM

DANCE SPACE:
Whole Class

Walking around the room, the children greet doors and windows. They salute the wall by making an upside-down shape against it. Sitting, they greet the floor by stroking it and bouncing on their bottoms; they promise to keep it clean for dancing. With upstretched arms they jump hello to the ceiling. This ritual begins to instill respect for their place of dance.

Problem J3

AUTO-STIMULATION

HOME SPACE:
Whole Class

Use your drumbeat to cut off each of the following exercises:

> **Walk and start breathing deep and hard.**
>
> **Stop and stand, looking down, breathing deep and hard.**
>
> **Run a few steps, stop and spin around, breathing hard and fast.**
>
> **Walk slowly, tired and dragging, breathing shallow, puffing.**

Discussion: What came into your mind as you did each part of the exercise? Did the way you were breathing stir up any particular feelings?

> **In this whisper exercise you shouldn't use real sentences. It's better if you use made-up sounds or nonsense words — it's just the soft, hissing, whispery noise that we want.**
>
> **Walk slowly, tiptoe, whispering.**
>
> **Kneel down and hunch over and whisper.**
>
> **Run and dodge and dart around, whispering.**
>
> **Run and freeze and whisper, fast as you can.**
>
> **In pairs on the floor, crawl together trading whispers.**

Discussion: as above.

Crouch down into a ball and scream.

Run screaming.

Stand with eyes shut and scream.

Discussion: A lot of young children love to scream, just in play.. But screaming sometimes means pain or fear or furious anger. Did you get any feelings from this exercise?

Have you seen one of those mechanical dolls as big as a grown-up at the Fun House? It looks like it's laughing. It jiggles and a kind of mechanical laughing sound comes out of a loudspeaker. See if you can do a laughing mechanical doll.

Stand and begin to snicker ... then chuckle ... then laugh out loud ... and louder and louder and throw your head back laughing ... and double up laughing ... and go down on the floor and roll over laughing.

Allow a little recovery time — deep breathing with eyes closed and a nice even drumming — and take this into ...

Lie flat on the floor and snore. A nice regular rhythm but getting softer and softer.

Making Faces

Living Masks

These exercises have nothing to do with playing an action complete with objectives, obstacles and givens. They pertain to stylized cartoon performance and should be used in conjunction with stylized movement, as in Problems D1 and D2.

Problem K1

FLEXING

HOME SPACE:
Whole Class

To the students:

Squish your face up as if you'd just bitten into a lemon; eyes smashed shut, mouth puckered up.

Now open your eyes big and your mouth wide and large.

Repeat three more times with small changes.

Isolating the facial parts:

Roll your eyeballs up into your forehead and down into your cheeks three times ... and side to side three times ... and blink as fast as you can 'til I say stop ... Stop.

Your mouth: pucker your lips as if sucking a gooey milkshake thru a straw ... grin - as big and wide as you can ... yawn - let it happen, wide wide open ...

167

snarl (show your teeth)... now snarl on your left
side ... now on your right.

Your cheeks: puff them out like a balloon. Release.
Again. Release.

Now just the right: mouth shut tight. Six puffs as
fast as you can. Now the left.

Eyebrows and forehead: down in a scowl — way
up wide-eyed — pulled in and — down in a frown
again ... and lift that frown upward with eyebrows
still pulled together — the worried look.

Your nose and upper lip sometimes work together
— Try pulling your nose over to the left. The
right. The left. The right. Crinkle your nose as if
there's a bad smell — crinkle five times. Flare
your nostrils four times (stretch them open as if
you need more air).

Problem K2 (of Set K2-K3)

STARTING TO MAKE THE MASK

THEATRE:
8 Players

To the Players, in a row facing the Audience:

Using mainly your mouth, express pain ... misery,
almost ready to cry ... joy ... controlled anger ...
contempt.

Using mainly your eyes, brows and forehead, show
astonishment ... rage ... puzzlement.

168

Discussion: You heard what those masks were meant to express. Did they succeed; did you get cartoons of human feelings?

Problem K3 (of Set K2-K3)

COMPLETING THE MASK

THEATRE:
8 Players

To the Players, in a row facing the Audience:

> **Let's start with expressionless faces — call it "neutral." I'll call out certain facial expressions. You make the mask and hold it until the drumbeat. Don't move your body.**
>
> **Weeping .... *[drumbeat]***
>
> **Coy, flirtatious .... *[drumbeat]***
>
> **Arrogant, sneering .. *[drumbeat]***
>
> **Shocked horror ...... *[drumbeat]***
>
> **Suspicious .... *[drumbeat]***
>
> **Laughing .... *[drumbeat]***

Discussion: as above. Did anyone notice that the mask of laughter could also be an expression of sudden intense pain, like having a door slam on your fingers? To make it surely a laughing mask, that mask needs sound or movement or a situation.

169

Problem K4 (of Set K4-K5)

MASKS WITH MOVEMENT

THEATRE:
Players in turn

To the Player:

> **Make you face into a mask, a cartoon of any feeling or mood you wish. Never change it during this problem.**

> **Now begin to improvise movements that seem to go with the mask.**

Discussion (after each Player): What mood did you see in the performance? Did the movements seem to go with the mask?

Repeat with other Players ad lib.

Problem K5 (of Set K4-K5)

MASKS AGAINST MOVEMENT

THEATRE:
Players in turn

This problem is extremely hard to do, but the class can have a lot of fun trying.

> **Assume a mask (the facial cartoon of a feeling) and don't change expression during the following action.**

> **Now begin to move — *but* the feeling expressed in the movement must be the opposite of the feeling on your face.**

Discussion: What feeling did you get from watching a face that said one thing and a body that contradicted it? Did you believe the face more than the body?

Problem K6 (of Set K6-K8)

DIALOGUE WITH MASKS 1

THEATRE:
Girl and Boy

When speaking, the Players are cool with neutral expressionless faces. When they stop talking the mask (showing their true feelings) snaps on.

Improv dialogue. He is trying to persuade her to cut class and hang out for a while. She is worried about cutting and about getting involved with him.

His mask is eager and seductive. Hers is worried and anxious. *[Action]*

Discussion: Did they concentrate and hold their masks when they weren't speaking? Which did you want to believe — what you heard or what you saw? — the words or the masks?

Problem K7 (of Set K6-K8)

DIALOGUE WITH MASKS 2

THEATRE:
3 Players

When speaking, the Players have blank neutral faces. When they stop speaking the mask appears.

The characters:

171

Secretary: **Tired, sad mask.**

Worker 1: **Suspicious mask.**

Worker 2: **Angry mask**

Situation: Workers have been called to the boss's office — they don't know why. Improv dialogue. They are wondering whether they'll be laid off or what. They try to pump the Secretary. No luck.

Drumbeat when they run out of steam.

Discussion: The scene needs an ending. Ask the class for ideas. Choose one and have the Players backtrack to a good starting point and play the suggested ending.

Problem K8 (of Set K6-K8)

DIALOGUE WITH MASKS 3

THEATRE:
3 Players

The characters:

Stranger: **Sinister mask.**

Student 1: **Pretend cool mask.**

Student 2: **Fearful mask.**

Situation: Students have just seen a stranger down the hall passing something to a student and taking some money in return. Is it a dope deal? The stranger comes toward them. Improv dialogue. Players take it from there.

If they come to no conclusion, stop them with a drumbeat.

Discussion: as above.

Motor Skills

The learning and cultivation of motor skills are of primal importance to the youngest of children in constructing a healthy self-image and a sense of ability. Hence most of the problems in this section of the Bank are meant for the preschool thru 2nd grade group, altho some problems which assume better-developed co-ordination are aimed at the higher grades.

Problem L1

GET READY TO DANCE

HOME SPACE:
Whole Class

Lead the class in this little song which helps preschoolers identify and feel distinctly the parts of their bodies. If you don't read music, improvise your own little tune:

Here's my ____ ,   It can dance,   See it mov-ing   thru the air!

As the song is sung, the children isolate different parts of their bodies, waving them toward the center of the circle.

As the children learn different parts of the song, let different students choose the next body part to "dance."

Problem L2

BODY PART WARM-UP

HOME SPACE:
Whole Class
Call out a body part you wish the child to shake, slowly or vigorously. At times have them freeze the body part into a shape. Then continue. At end of this isolation warm-up have the children shake their whole bodies.

Problem L3 (of Set L3-L4)

THE MAGIC EYE 1

HOME SPACE:
Whole Class
If Magic Eye exercises haven't yet been introduced explain that each child has a Magic Eye — a very private and personal make-believe thing that has special powers. It's located in the middle of chest. Inspect each Magic Eye and ask its color.

> **Hide your Magic Eye by rounding your backs.**
>
> **Release (lift up) and show me your Magic Eye.**

Repeat once or twice.

> **Shake and twist your Magic Eye.**
>
> **Share it with your neighbor on your right side ... and on your left side.**
>
> **Collapse and hide it again.**

Problem L4 (of Set L3-L4)

MAGIC EYE 2

DANCE SPACE:
Whole Class

Select appropriate music (See page 39 Music Suggestions)
To the children:

>**Take the Magic Eye and whirl it around.**
>
>**Slide it along the floor.**
>
>**Close your eyes and listen to your Magic Eye. I think it wants you to ....**
>
>**... open your eyes and get up and dance on tippy-toes — arms high, reaching up ... and running ... and** *[drumbeat]* **collapse to the floor and hide your Magic Eye.**

Repeat.

Problem L5

THE WEATHER GAME

HOME SPACE:
Whole Class

Seat the children in a circle.

>**Tap your toes lightly on the floor to make rain.** *[action]*
>
>**Shoot your arms or legs forward and back to make lightning - "tchew! tchew!"** *[action]*

Do rain again ... *[action]* ... and bang fast on the floor with your feet to make thunder.

Repeat rain, lightning and thunder.

Make sunshine. Stretch your legs out and put your arms up like this *[5th position]*. Turn from side to side to warm your neighbors.

Repeat rain, lightning, thunder and sunshine twice. Then, with arms up in sunshine attitude, have the children move into the Dance Space for their next problem.

Note: the Weather Exercise may equally well be done standing and in the Dance Space to music.

Problem L6

SOW BUG

**DANCE SPACE:
Whole Class**

Discuss the sow bug if you can. If any of the children know of it, have them describe it..

Let's pretend we're tiny little bugs about this big *[show 1/4 of an inch]* that can curl itself up into tight little balls. *[action]*

Now let's roll onto our backs and open up — quick! *[action]* and wave all our arms and legs in the air *[action]*.

Now quickly — everyone curl up again.

Repeat.

176

Sow bugs also can crawl when they're halfway curled up ... *[action]* ... Now stop and curl up tight ... *[action]*.

Roll over and wave in the air again. *[action]*

Crawl slowly on elbows and knees, head down low ... crawl around and then curl up tight again *[action]* ... and

roll over and wave in the air again!

Problem L7 (of Set L7-L8)

THE FISHING EXERCISE

HOME SPACE: Whole Class

This exercise cultivates isolation of foot and stomach movements, hamstring stretches and thigh muscle development.

The children sit in a circle with their feet extended toward the center. Lead them thru a directed fantasy:

Wave and wiggle your feet. They look like little fish ... look at them swimming.

Take a fishing pole with both hands and cast the fish line far out into the pond *[the center of the circle. Their hands are now out beyond their feet].*

Pull them in. Grab the fish! ... *[bringing the feet up to the crotch with knees winged out sideways].*

They're going to swim into the pond again!

> **Go after them ...** *[repeat 3, 4 and 5 a few times and then ...]*
>
> **Now let's eat them and see if they can swim around in our tummies** *[a quick gulp is all].*

The children undulate their stomach muscles; they show rather than tell you how the fish are swimming within. Go from child to child, commenting on the various ways in which the fish seem to be swimming.

> **Now give a big burp and your tummy will be flat again.**

Problem L8 (of Set L7-L8)

STRENGTHENING-LIMBERING

HOME SPACE:
Whole Class

The children sit on the floor in a circle and ....

With legs crossed in approximate lotus position, have them round the torso over to look at the floor with their Magic Eyes.

With legs straight in front in first position they round over to look at their knees with their Magic Eyes.

With legs crossed again, turn the Magic Eye from side to side and bend to show it the floor on either side.

"Make a bridge." With hands and feet flat on the floor and arms and legs bent, the children arch their backs as high as they can, so that a tall ship can sail under the bridge.

The bridge is transformed into a bear. Stiff-legged, the bears parade in a circle, stretching their hamstrings.

Trees are swaying in the wind. The children's arms are the branches. Have the children face full front (no twisting) during these lateral stretches. First the East Wind blows, then the West Wind, then East again, rhythmically.

The cat is asleep, all curled up. Slowly it wiggles its back and rises onto its hands and knees. Its back is straight. It stretches its hind legs, one after the other, as far out and high up as it can.

It sees a dog. Up goes its back in a high arch and kitty cat hisses as loud as it can.

The dog disappears. The cat lies down on its side and stretches all four legs out as far as it can, with a nice back bend ... and then curls up and goes back to sleep.

Problem L9 (of Set L9-L11)

IMAGINATION

DANCE SPACE
Whole Class

To the students:

> **The bears walk around the room, arms and legs stiff, and then ... roll over on your backs *[drum]* Look at that! You've turned into a lion! She's resting in the grass, waving her tail up in the air. Make one of your legs into a tail and wave it ... and bring it down slowly ... and now Ms. Lion is getting sleepy ... so curl up ... and shut your eyes ... and we'll play *sleepyhead.***

Problem L10 (of Set L9-L11)

SLEEPYHEAD

DANCE SPACE: **Pretend to be asleep. But when I come and touch you, open your eyes — sssssshhhh, not a sound ... go tiptoe to where I point.**

Direct them one by one into a circle around the last slumberer; lead them in a soft chant:

"Sleephead, Sleepyhead, Wake up, get out of bed."

Help Sleepyhead up. Sleepyhead leads the others in a line around the room, while they mime every movement Sleepyhead makes. *Drumbeat* to end the routine.

Note: Music can be used for both the Imagination and Sleepyhead exercises. Here are some suggestions:

Bartok *"For Children: Book 1"*, side 1, bank 4 (first part)

Kabalevsky *"24 Preludes"* , side 1, cut 2 *"Scherzando"*

Joe Pass & Paulinho da Corta *Tudo Bem*, side 2, *"Que que ha"*

Debussy *Children's Corner Suite,* band 8, *"Berceuse des Elephantes"*

Problem L11 (of Set L9-L11)

MISTER FALL-DOWN

DANCE SPACE
Whole Class

Select music with a simple clear structure and phrases with obvious endings, so that the children begin link movement to music, falling as the musical phrase comes to an end.

Explain that Mr. Fall-down never falls on his knees or elbows, but always on his butty-wutt or thigh. Have the children practice falling backwards and sideways, and then, with music:

> **Run and run** *[with the musical passage]* **and run and** *[musical phrase ends]* **be Mr. Fall-down!**

> *[As above]* **Turn and turn and turn — be Mr. Fall-down!**

> *[As above]* **Run and run and jump! Jump! Jump! and be Mr. Fall-down!**

This exercise may be extended into floor-level locomotor movements by issuing added commands with the fall-down, eg. " — be a Mr. Falldown and crawl sideways" (or "move forward on your butty-wutt," "crawl backwards," "roll over and over").

Problem L12

DANCE SPACE
Half the Class

Drumming the appropriate rhythm helps with some of these locomotor movements, but with some just a light vibrato to indicate duration is best. Call out the following:

walk	**walk on all fours**
crawl	**jump, feet together**
roll	**cartwheels**
bounce	**march**
crawl on back	**slide**
stagger	**trot**
run	**leap**
skip	**travel as you turn**
hop	**frog leaps**
gallop	**somersaults**

Repeat with the other half the class.

Change the quality of the natural movements by introducing imagery. Have the children:

walk barefoot on ice	**step *over* logs in a row**
walk on logs in a row	**walk on a tightrope**

walk in deep sticky mud   walk in deep water

walk on a springy mattress   walk on a cloud

travel like a frisbee in the air

Problem L13

LOCOMOTOR RHYTHMS & PHRASES

THEATRE:
11 Players

Divide the class into three groups, taking turns performing.

1st group to do the following:

> **Skip** *[4 beats]* **... slow motion walk** *[4 beats]* **... hop** *[2 beats]* **... jump** *[1 beat].*

Repeat; keep it flowing this time around.

2nd group demonstrates the slide and leap:

> **Slide** *[4 beats]* **... slow motion walk** *[2 beats]* **... leap** *[3 beats].*

Repeat for flow.

3rd group demonstrates gallop:

> **Gallop** *[4 beats]* **... slow motion walk** *[3 beats]* **... fall down** *[1 beat].*

Repeat as above.

Problem L14

LOCOMOTOR SKILLS

DANCE SPACE
Quartets in turn

Place a drumstick or line of shoes in the center of the floor and have the quartet in unison ...

> **run and jump backwards over the "line."**

> **run and jump, making an airborne shape over the "line."**

"Erase" the line; instead, hold a drumstick about two feet off the floor and have the students, one at a time:

> **run and go under the stick by rolling, crawling, sliding on tummy or back, etc.**

Problem L15

BALL GAME

THEATRE:
A Third of the Class

To the Players:

> **You have an imaginary ball. The game is to bounce it around to different parts of your body without using your hands — elbow, foot, shoulder, knee, head, whatever — without using your hands.**

> **Choose three places on your body. Show me the first and I'll toss the ball to it. Catch it, balance it, roll it around and bounce it gently ... and flip it to the next body part.**

Demonstrate. For example: back of hand to opposite elbow to foot.

Students perform, two at a time.

Retire the Players and send the rest of the class up to perform two at a time as partners.

Now the game is the same as above except that Partner Number 1, after catching and manipulating the ball on the third body part, flips it to Partner 2.

Partner 2 catches it on a selected body part and goes thru the same exercise, ending with a flip back to Partner 1. End of duet.

Repeat with other twosomes.

Problem L16

RANDOM CONTINUOUS MOTION

THEATRE:
Half the Class

To the students:

> **When the drumming begins start moving and don't stop. Use any kind of motion that comes into your head. You needn't use your whole body ... you can use a part, change to the whole body ... change to another part ... or stay with one part ... just keep moving without pause.**

Druming softly throughout. *Drumbeat* to stop.

Discussion: Did it seem frantic, or were there some parts when it got quieter? Did anyone relate to anyone else, as if they were playing together?

Repeat with the other half the class. Do the same exercise with music (something with a sense of continuous motion). *Drumbeat* to stop.

Discussion: Could you tell whether they were using the rhythm and tempo of the music?

Repeat with the other half the class.

Do the same exercise in silence. Repeat with the other half the class.

Discussion: How did it feel to do it in silence, compared to drumming or music?

Problem L17

Body awareness: kinesthesia, or the kinetic sense, is the agency which molds gross motor competence into controlled expressiveness.

TRAVELING MOVEMENTS

THEATRE:
10 Players

To the students:

> **There's energy in you ... and if you think hard you can feel it waiting in any part of you you're concentrating on. It's waiting to flow from one place to another, moving your body parts as it flows along.**

Move your fingers; start a movement impulse that travels to your

    elbow ... then to your

    back

    foot

    leg

    tummy

    other leg

    fingers

Discussion (to the audience): Could you see the energy flow from one part to another? Did it seem to keep going, or stop and start?

Repeat with other Players - this time, add music with a definite pulse.

Objectives, Obstacles & Givens

Acting is make-believe and make-believe needs imagination. Imagination in drama is guided and stimulated by three specific guide posts: the *objective* : what the character (or animal) is trying to do right at that moment. And the *obstacle* : something that stands in the way, altho there's always hope that it can be overcome. And the *givens* : the situation, the environment — everything that influences the way in which the objective is pursued. In the problems for the very young these factors are spelled out — a road map into the realm of fantasy. But with continuing exercise of the imagination the children can invent their own objectives, obstacles and givens.

Problem M1

INVENTIONS

THEATRE:
7 Players in turn

To Player 1:

> **A hurricane wind is blowing thru the door.**
>
> **Objective: shut the door.**
>
> **Obstacle: power of the wind.**
>
> **Given (limitation): you may push with only three body parts, one at a time. Monologue if you wish; repeat the same phrase throughout the scene.**
>
> **To end the scene: achieve your objective and slide exhausted down the doorframe to the floor.**

To Player 2:

Do the same problem, but select another limitation and another ending.

To Player 3:

You slipped while hiking and your foot is caught in a tough, thorny bush — jammed between branches.

Objective: to get free.

Obstacle: thorns. Jerk and you get stabbed. Reach in and you get pricked. Monologue if you wish; repeat the same phrase throughout the scene.

Given: You have a sharp pocket knife.

Invent an ending.

To Player 4:

It's one a.m. and you were supposed to be home at 10 o'clock. If you get caught you're in deep trouble. You've sneaked up onto the back porch.

Objective: slip in thru the back window.

Obstacles: the window is sticky and jams after you get it started. There are glasses lined up on the window sill inside, ready to fall and crash if you bump them.

Given: there are various items on the back porch. Invent and use anything you need.

Invent an ending.

To Player 5:

> **Same objective and obstacles, but use a different way of trying to overcome the obstacle. Invent a different ending.**

To Players 6 and 7:

> **You're in a situation together; take a few minutes to discuss it. Develop it in detail.**
>
> **It is a situation in which there is a strong force working on you — pulling you, pushing you, or dragging you down. You decide what, where it is and what it's like.**
>
> **You try to resist it, but it's hard because of some other obstacle. What?**
>
> **Select one or more givens; it (they) can be either an advantage or a disadvantage to you.**
>
> **Invent an ending.**
>
> **Talk to each other while you struggle.**

Problem M2

GROUP IMPROVISATIONS

THEATRE: To the students:
Class in Groups
of 5 — 7

As a group invent a simple situation — if possible, one with conflict.

Each member of a group is to decide what character you are to be.

Each member in a group is to decide on an objective — what it is you want in your scene. Several members may share the same objective.

As a group, define the obstacles and the givens of your situation. Use dialogue if desired.

Follow each performance with an evaluation: Was the situation clear? Did it have a point of conflict? Were the characters and their objectives clear to you? If not, why? what went wrong? What were the obstacles? Were they hard to overcome? Did you believe the situation? If not, why? What would have made it more believable?

Problem M3

IMPROVISATION

**THEATRE:
Class in Groups
of 5 — 7**

Have each group invent a situation, one with elements of conflict or difficulty. Each student invents a character and an objective. The group defines the obstacles and the givens of the situation. Use dialogue if desired.

Problem M4

THEATRE:
Players 4 — 6

King Zap is auditioning servants for high-paying jobs at the Palace. The applicants either get hired or zapped (vaporized on the spot).

Applicants:

Objective: **to please the King.**

Obstacle: **who knows what does?**

Given: **they can make three tries to please.**

King Zap:

Objective: **to find servants who please him no matter what they do.**

Obstacle: **he may run out of applicants by over-zapping**

Given: **no zapping until during or after the third try.**

King Zap sits on one side of the stage. Applicants stand in a row on the other. One by one they come to the King and make whatever efforts to please the Player selects.

Examples (for use if the student draws a blank):

Dance for him   Flatter him

Shine his shoes   Sing for him

193

Give him a shave   Tell jokes

The king asks questions; there is dialogue.

A zapped applicant collapses into a crouch and instantly rushes back to the applicants' row.

If the king is pleased, the exercise is over or may be repeated with a new King Zap.

This problem can be made contemporary:

Employer is laying off workers. One comes in with the objective of keeping his/her job.

Highway Patrol stops a speeding driver, who tries to avoid getting a ticket.

Oral Expressiveness

The following exercises help over-come shyness and make communication more telling by conscious choices of emphasis, tempo, contrast. They are useful for all young children and they have special value for those for whom English is a second language.

Problem N1

MOVING WITH WORDS

THEATRE:
Half the Class

To the students:

> **Our first travel path is a circle — a *big* circle. You're to jog around it while you say, over and over again, "Mary had a little lamb." The first drumbeat means "Start," and the second drumbeat means "Stop."** *[Drum ... drum]* **Excellent.**

One Player up, positioned UL.

> **Your travel path will take you over there** *[point to DR]* **— that's called a *diagonal* path, slanting from up left where you're standing to down right. Skip and say "Mary had a little pig." Drum means "Start" and drum means "stop."** *[Drum ... drum]*

Five players up in a row upstage.

> **Your travel path is straight down toward the audience and you're twirling like tops as you come, and you're shouting, "Mary had a little pig." Drum to start; drum to stop.** *[Drum ... drum]*

Eight Players up in two ranks of four, side by side, DR facing L (: : : :).

> Your travel path is cross stage and your movement is marching. You'll be saying, "Mary had a big pet frog." Begin marching without moving forward, like this *[demonstrate]*. I'll count like this: "Left two three four," so that everyone is together. When I hit the drum, start across the stage, saying "Mary had a big pet frog," and stop when I drum again. Left, two three four, left two three *[drum]* left*[etc., and ... drum]*.

Two Players:

> Now let's combine a travel path with saying a word plus moving some part of you body to show what you're feeling when you *say* the word. *[One player at a time.]*

Player A: Your travel path is: Diagonal UR to DL

Your locomotor movement is: Walking

Your body part is: Head

Your voice is saying: "No" over and over

Player B: Travel path: Circle

Locomotor movement: Running

Body part: Arms waving overhead

Word: "Wait" over and over

Two Players. They are both to be in continuous motion, but they take turns speaking, one *right after* the other. Player One, doing a serpentine path, avoids collision with Player Two, whose pattern is more rigid.

196

Player 1: Travel path: **Serpentine, UL to DR, slowly**

Locomotor movement: **Shuffle, tiny steps**

Body parts: **Arms hugging tummy**

Voice: **"I've got a belly ache"**

Player 2: Travel path: **Square**

Locomotor movement: **Walk backwards**

Body parts: **Arms, beating chest**

Voice: **"It's cold in this room"**

If there is time, repeat with other players and have them invent their own paths, actions and words.

Discussion: Students comment on what was hard, what was easy, whether the words influenced the action, etc.

Problem N2

VOWEL, CONSONANT SOUNDS AND MOVEMENT

HOME SPACE:
Whole Class

In a circle. Call on one student to vocalize a vowel or consonant sound, then follow it with a simple movement. Class then imitates 1st student's sound and movement.

Call a 2nd student, who does a different vowel/consonant sound and movement. Class again imitates, then quickly repeats 1st and 2nd in succession. After 3rd; repeat 1st, 2nd, and 3rd, etc.

Keep on building the sequence, each time repeating all the sounds and movements in succession. See if you can build sequence to 10.

An add-on: Ask any volunteer in the circle to make a *non-language* voice-sound — any kind of noise the voice can make — accompanied by simultaneous movements. The class imitates in unison. Continue with other volunteers (up to 4, if they come fast).

Problem N3

SPEAK AND DO 1

HOME SPACE:
Whole Class

Demonstrate to the class what they are to do: perform an action and describe it as it is being performed. Speak and do.

I lift up my arms. Higher! *[Class imitates]*

I turn around twice. *[Class imitates]*

I step sideways. *[Class imitates]*

SPEAK
AND DO 2

THEATRE:
1 Several Players

A few students in turn make up and perform their own sets of four verbalized actions.

SPEAK
AND DO 3

THEATRE:
4 Players

Arrange the Players thus:

        1   2

3   4

      Audience

Player 1 invents a speak-&-do. Player 2 imitates it and adds another. Player 3 imitates both and adds a third. Player 4 imitates the preceding three and adds a fourth.

Problem N4

SENTENCE MODULATION

HOME SPACE:
Whole Class

These games show how, by juggling accents, pauses and energy levels, a sentence can convey two or more messages, all at the same time. The messages might be:

      simple information or request
      a feeling about delivering the message

      a feeling about the person being addressed

      certainty or uncertainty about the message

      Illustrate with a simple sentence like this:

      Flat disinterested: **Polly's mad and I'm glad.**

      Selected accents: **Polly's mad and I'm GLAD!**

Selected pauses: **Polly's — mad, and — I'm — glad.**

One Player repeats the above example.

Another Player give three readings of this:

Polly's really mad but really I don't care — so there!

Eight Players in turn do the following lines using combined accents and pauses in two different readings. Before speaking, the Player should imagine a context: whom is being addressed and what's the situation. After each performance let the Watchers discuss what the speaker's feelings were in each version.

1st Player: **Tomorrow is another day.**

2nd Player: **Relax your arms, wrists and fingers.**

3rd Player: **Hey, it's just part of the scene.**

4th Player: **I was absolutely weightless.**

5th Player: **Look who's coming!**

6th Player: **Well, we can do it too.**

7th Player: **Today I'm feeling kind of sick.**

8th Player: **I've gotta surprise for you.**

Sixteen Players, working in pairs. Basically the same exercise as above, this version is more fun for the class because it involves a kind of bizarre dialogue. Player 1 says a line;

Player 2 responds with the second line. Player 1 repeats the first line but with different accents and pauses. Player 2 answers with a new reading of the second line. Same pattern for all couples.

Watchers should look for a difference in feelings between the first and second readings of each sentence. Discuss after each pair performs. Did they seem to talk to each other or just be thinking private thoughts?

Player 1:   **Relax your arms, wrists and fingers.**

Player 2:   **Tomorrow is another day.**

Player 1:   **Relax** etc. *[different reading]*

Player 2:   **Tomorrow** etc. *[different reading]*

Player 3:   **Today I'm feeling kind of sick.**

Player 4:   **Hey, it's part of the scene.**
[Repeat as above]

Player 5:   **I was absolutely weightless.**

Player 6:   **Well, we can do it too.**
[Repeat as above]

Player 7:   **Hey, look who's coming.**

Player 8:   **I've got a big surprise for you.**
[Repeat as above]

Player 9:   **It's funny how things change.**

Player 10:   **I told him he had four arms and he agreed.**
[Repeat as above]

Player 11:   **Will you be my Valentine?**

Player 12:   **Funny, I can't think of a thing.**
[Repeat as above]

Player 13:   **This fruit is too green.**

Player 14:   **Are all things the same, or does it matter?**
[Repeat as above]

Player 15:   **I'm lost without my keys.**

Player 16:   **Times are hard and friends are few.**
[Repeat as above]

Problem N5 (of Set N5-N6)

WORDS, ACTION AND ENERGY 1

THEATRE:
Groups of 6

Six sentences are involved. Let the class repeat them until they are memorized (a blackboard would help). 6 Players perform in turn. Each Player says his/her line in the following ways:

(a) with a free, natural, expressive gesture.

(b) with great energy and big, vigorous gesture.

(c) with the same feeling of energy, but no physical movement at all.

Player 1:   **Relax your arms, hands and fingers.**

Player 2:	I haven't heard, I do not know, I cannot guess, I do not care — OK?
Player 3:	I'll never believe that rotten lie, you rotten bum.
Player 4:	I don't love you but I sure like you — I do, I do.
Player 5:	If you poison us do we not die? and if you wrong us shall we not revenge?
Player 6:	C'mon, man, gimme a break — I'm hungry, cold and broke.

Discussion: Which of the three ways of speaking seemed the most powerful? Was the same true of all six sentences? Was anybody real and believable in all three styles?

Problem N6 (of Set N5-N6)

WORDS, ACTION, ENERGY 2

THEATRE:
Pairs

The Players perform a few improvised lines, an interchange in the 3 styles (a, b, and c) described in the preceding problem. Let them perform in two imagined situations:

A greeting between friends who haven't seen each other for a long time.

An argument between two not-so-friendly friends about who owns a schoolbook lying on the floor.

Problem N7

THEATRE:
Groups of 4 or 5

Each group is to invent a situation in which each Player has a single sentence. They will need a little time to work the problem out.

Example: Post Office window, with a Postal clerk, a customer who's asking a long stupid question, a customer who's in a big hurry, and a tired, cranky janitor.

The scene is to be done 3 times, in the 3 styles (a, b and c) described in Problem N 3 above. The Players must concentrate on their objectives and on each other, and not interrupt another's speech.

Physical Expressiveness

Qualities of Movement

In dance art-forms, movement quality replaces the inflections of the human voice. It is synonymous with expressiveness. The way one moves induces feeling in the performer and conveys feeling to the watchers. The aim of these exercises is to reveal and to elaborate the different qualities of movement. Your voice will be a dynamic element ...... vocal qualities suggest movement qualities.

Problem O1

THE BASIC QUALITIES 1

DANCE SPACE
Whole Class

For good descriptive language on the five major kinds of movement see Chap. VI, Model Class Plan 2

As you describe the movement qualities, tell your students to feel the energy flow, the amount and kind of energy needed for each. Demonstrate each and let the class mirror your movement:

> **Sustained.**   **Slow even energy output.**
>
> **Percussive.**   **Abruptly released, abruptly checked.**
>
> **Swinging.**   **Initial impulse, follow-thru and fall back.**
>
> **Vibratory.**   **Continuous, strong, tightly-confined energy release.**

Suspended. Hanging at the moment of change from balance to imbalance ... then ... a drop-thru and recovery.

THE BASIC
QUALITIES 2

DANCE SPACE
Half the Class

Call out the qualities in varying order, making your voice an expressive instrument to convey the feeling of the movement type. Try using the drum, too, for dynamic effect.

Repeat with the other half the class, using music appropriate to each quality.

Discussion: what movements in ordinary life, whether human, animal or mechanical, have any of these five movement qualities?

Problem 02 (of Set 02-05)

CONTRASTS 1

THEATRE:
10 Players

Black / white ... soft / sharp ... big / small ... sweet / sour ... loud / silent ... cloudy / clear ... no performance is interesting without contrast.

Let's look at some contrasting movement qualities. Players, select any movement but perform it with the quality I call out.

Percussive (sharp).   **Sustained (smooth)**

Vibrating (bubbly).   **Swinging (rhythmic)**

Suspended (stop-action) Percussive (sharp)

206

Discussion: What was the difference in energy output for percussive and sustained? For vibrating and swinging? For suspended and percussive?

Repeat with other groups until the whole class has had turns.

Problem O3 (of Set O2-O5)

CONTRASTS 2

THEATRE:
3 Players

The Players stand about six feet apart in a row. They perform at the same time but independently. Give them a minute to each select a pair of contrasting movements.

They are to begin with one movement and transition into the other.

Take examples, if required, from O2, above.

Discussion: Which two qualities did [Player's name] show us? ...and the others? Which set of movements showed the most contrast? What made it more contrasting? more energy contrast? tempo contrast? range [bigness] contrast? Which transition was smoothest and worked best?

Problem O4 (of Set O2-O5)

CONTRASTS 3

THEATRE:
2 Players

To Player 1:

On the drumbeat, enter and begin to perform any movement you like with whatever movement quality you choose. You may change the *movement* if you want, but keep the same *quality* — if it's swinging, stick with swinging, for instance.

To Player 2:

I'll drum 20 soft beats during that performance. Watch it carefully and choose a *contrasting* movement quality. I'll give you a cue to enter — a loud double drumbeat.

They will continue until you stop them.

Discussion: was there good contrast between them? Would you say the contrast came more from a difference in tempo, or range, or energy — or just feeling? How was their concentration?

Problem 05 (of Set 02-05)

CONTRASTS 4

THEATRE:
Trios in turn

To the Players:

We'll do this problem in 32 beats.

Player 1 improvises a series of quick, sharp percussive movements.

Player 2 improvises off-balance suspension movements. These can vary from slow motion to moderately fast.

Player 3 walks and stops to focus offstage for a few beats — then walks again and stops to take some other focus.

On beat 30, I'll call "30!" and everyone stops, turns, walks toward the audience and bows. *[Action]*

Discussion: There were two kinds of contrast there: one, between two different movement qualities ... and one between active movement and stillness. Which one was the stronger contrast (think back to what you mostly looked at)?

Problem 06

DUETS

THEATRE:
Pairs in turn

This duet is a 24-count passage consisting of three 8-count. parts. Drum lightly to synchronize the Players.

To the Players:

Part 1 — 8 beats. Player 1: take a placement, take a focus and stand still. Player 2: create a movement with one of the 5 basic qualities.

Part 2 — 8 beats. Player 1: move to a new place and invent a movement with one of the 5 qualities. Player 2: change to a new quality.

Part 3 — Player 1: stop, take a focus and freeze. Player 2: go back to the original Part 1 movement.

I'll call out beats "8," "16" and "Cut."

Discussion: Did you see anything interesting? Did it seem anything like a dance with a beginning, a middle and an end? How was their concentration? What movement qualities did you see?

Problem 07

SOUND QUALITY/ MOVEMENT QUALITY

HOME SPACE:
All

Discuss how feelings can be communicated by (1) voice quality (tone of voice) and (2) movement quality and also by (3) non-verbal sound quality. Everyone knows that music stimulates feeling, but what about everyday sounds and noises?

Do they? Ask the students what they think.

Let's do an exercise in which I'll call out the name of a sound, like "siren," and you match it with a movement quality — for siren, it would be the sustained quality, perhaps with a rising gesture.

Sounds (try to sound like them)   Matching movement

bang	**percussive, explosive**
pop	**percussive, startling**
kerrrplunk	**suspended and drop**
(phone) ring	**sustained**
church bell	**swinging**
dog growl	**sustained**
hiccough	**percussive**
giggle	**vibratory**

210

Now that they have the idea, do the list again.

Divide the class into two groups. Let them line up facing each other.

The child at the top of the line on the left calls out a sound — any sound, either by name or by vocalizing it.

The person opposite responds with a matching movement quality.

So on down the line. At the bottom the roles are reversed; the responder now becomes the caller and the game progresses back up to the top.

Problem 08

A SCENE

**THEATRE:
Five Players**

Set up the improvisation by establishing where the curb and street are. Decide from which direction the bus is to pass. Then brief each Player.

To the Players:

> **You're waiting for a bus on a cold, windy street corner. Player 1 and Player 2, you've forgotten your sweaters and coats. Do what you can to keep warm. Player 3 you're being pestered by a nagging fly. Do what you can, but it just won't go away. Player 4, you're in a hurry so you stand on the edge of the curb, leaning out over the street to catch sight of the bus. And Player 5, you're a grown-up in no hurry. You just pace up and down patiently.**

211

I'll give you all 20 drum beats to play out the scene.

Action.

Discussion: What movement qualities did the audience see? Ask them to identify each one. Were all the Players concentrating on the problem? Could the audience imagine the street corner? Did they seem like strangers or did it seem they knew one another? Were some or all of the Players aware of the audience? If yes, how could you tell?

Try another group. You may wish to include dialogue this time. Coach your Players not to *show* us their cold or annoyance at the fly. Tell them just to concentrate on where they are and what they're doing. This may keep them from over-acting and being self-conscious and aware of the audience.

Problem 09

THE FOUR ANCIENT ELEMENTS

THEATRE: To the students:

In ancient times it was thought that there were only four elements: earth, water, air and fire. Let's express, in body movement, the essential quality of each element.

Become a person whose quality of movement is that of air, water, fire or earth. Each of those elements has various aspects. So choose a specific one.

Earth: **massive ... solid ... dense**

212

Water:	flowing ... dripping ... surging ... rippling
Air:	light ... breezy ... swirling ... gusty ... storm-windy
Fire:	roaring ... flickering ... smoldering

The very challenging problem is for the student to perform the following tasks "in the person of" one of the elements. There are four tasks:

Hanging out the washing   **Raking leaves**

Doing calisthenics   **Washing the car**

Preparation: the student should concentrate, with eyes closed, selecting an element and an *aspect* of the element to "be"—to try to feel like squishy sticky mud or a flickering flame, for instance, and keep that feeling going while pantomiming the action. The student announces the element.

If too many choices fall on one or two elements, suggest or assign others.

Call out the tasks, allowing at least a full minute for each (more if the Player seems deeply involved).

Pause after every third or fourth performance, for:

Discussion (to Players): Did you feel as if your personality had changed for a few minutes? Was it really possible to feel like the element you selected? (to Watchers) — Did the actions seem a little more unusual and interesting when they were done this way?

213

Props

Using Objects to Stimulate Imagination

These problems grow out of the games young children play, in which two chairs and a blanket become a cave or a straddled broom becomes a horse. Literal reality becomes a springboard to other visions. Your problem is to provide the props. Get next to the school custodian, the maestro of the brooms, mops, milk crates, ladders, pails. Chairs are versatile. Rope, small tarps, fabric, bicycle tires, umbrellas, cartons, hula hoops ... the list is long (but stay away from items too tiny to be clearly visible to the audience). Place them along the sides of the stage area.

Problem P1 (of Set P1-P3)

MAKE-BELIEVE 1

THEATRE:
Third of the Class
Each student in turn chooses an object and, by pantomime, converts it into something else. Eg., a chair becomes a ticket window, or a bathtub, or (tilted back and pushed along on two legs) a shopping cart.

Give them a little time. The readiest goes first.

Discussion (promptly, after each): What was it? How was the concentration? What was the action that told you what it was?

Problem P2 (of Set P1-P3)

MAKE-BELIEVE 2

THEATRE:
10 new Players

Problem P1 is now extended. The Player picks a prop that can be manipulated for some time (at least a full minute). Eg., a broom becomes a hard rock singer's guitar and the action is a parody of the singer's performance contortions.

Or the prop becomes something that simply stimulates a strong reaction that can be played out for a   minute — anxiety, curiosity, temptation. Eg., a rope becomes a snake; a bike tire becomes a fountain into which people have tossed coins that might be swiped.

The problem's purpose is to evoke sense memory and action recall. Action may be small or large, busy or deliberate — but must be without long pauses.

Discussion: Did the Player find more than one thing to do with the prop? Did the action interest you? Can you think of other ways the image-object might be handled or used?

Problem P3 (of Set P1-P3)

MAKE-BELIEVE 3

THEATRE:
Class in groups
of 5

This problem calls for 4 or 5 props per group, altho they needn't all be different. A group might have four chairs and a pail, for instance. Obviously a scarcity of props will limit the number of groups that can work simultaneously.

The problem: by using props as make-believe objects, to create a specific place, an environment in which the action takes place. Eg., machines in a factory; action in a playground.

Distribute the props and position the groups around the room so that they can confer privately. Give them a minute, then visit them in turn to help those that haven't agreed on a "place."

They perform in turn, with the others as audience.

Problem P4

NEXT CLASS

HOMEWORK: The problem:

> **Bring something to class that you've practiced with and perform for us. It's fine to use two or more props if you wish — the object you bring plus a chair or two here, for instance.**

You or the home-room teacher should give the children a reminder before the next session.

Rhythm and Sound

These problems are arranged in approximate order of ascending grade levels, beginning with Problem 1 for pre-K; Q2 for K and 1st; adding Q4 for 2nd grade thru 4th, and Q6 thru Q9 for 5th thru 8th grades.

Problem Q1 (of Set Q1-Q3)

LEARNING THE BEAT

HOME SPACE:
Whole Class

Children sit cross-legged in a circle. Drumming lightly and counting loudly, you establish a marching beat — an unstressed "ONE ONE ONE ONE" etc. The children clap in time to the beat.

Repeat with different rhythms: ONE, ONE *two* ...or ONE *two three* (waltz time) ... or ONE *two three four* ... and (double downbeat) ONE TWO *three four five six*. (Any repeated pattern of accented and unaccented makes a rhythm, of course, but don't get too fancy at first). Have the children count aloud and accent the downbeat with various body parts: elbows, head, feet, torso, knee, etc.

HEARING THE RHYTHM

DANCE SPACE:
Whole Class

Select appropriate music (dances are easiest). The children walk to the music, turning, zigzagging or improvising their floor patterns, but always accenting the downbeat. Use the drum only if the students seem confused about the rhythm.

Problem Q2 (of Set Q1-Q3)

RHYTHM STUDIES

HOME SPACE:
Whole Class

The drum is passed from child to child, and each child beats out the syllables of its name ("Su—san—Wil—kins"). Hand-claps can substitute for the drum if necessary.

Each child in turn chants its name, clapping or body-slapping a two-beat rhythm:

"My [rest] **name is Ju-lius Jones**" [rest]
  1   2   1 2 1 2   1   2

Problem Q3 (of Set Q1-Q3)

CLIMBING THE LADDER

DANCE SPACE:
Whole Class

To the students:

> **Let's practice the 3-beat. Pretend you're climbing a stepladder. You must be slow and careful. Take a step each time I hit the drum. When you get to the top I'll say "You're up!" ... but then you lose your balance and fall down and start up again.**

Count slowly and drum to accent the down beat.

Problem Q4

THE GIFT

THEATRE:
6 to 8 Players

Pre-select music with an obvious rhythm.

> **When the music begins, you will begin to move. Move any way you want, but keep the rhythm — stamp or clap on the downbeat. Your movement will be called "the Gift" and you are going to fly your own airplane and take your gift anywhere in the world you want.**

Action. Once the students have established their rhythmic actions, call a halt and "wrap the gift" — tie an imaginary ribbon around whatever body part each child chooses. Then direct them to their aircraft, which are parked around the edges of the Theatre Space. Ask each one what country or city or even street address s/he will fly to.

> **You can be any kind of aircraft you want — airplane or helicopter or even a bird. Ready for take-off? Take off and fly!**

Bring them down in an easy descent and landing and let each child announce the location and the fact that the gift has been delivered. If a map is at hand, show the fliers where they have brought their gifts.

Problem Q5

TEMPO

DANCE SPACE:
Whole Class

Establish a "race track" around the Dance Space and a travel direction (eg., clockwise). Introduce the word "tempo." Class is to run to a tempo set by your drumming. It will change across a variety of speeds.

The children skip to a slow two-beat skipping rhythm (DUM ta-DUM ta-DUM ta-DUM). The drumming accelerates and retards them again, varying but always maintaining each tempo long enough for the child to feel it kinesthetically.

Problem Q6

CHOOSING RHYTHM AND TEMPO

THEATRE:
2 Players

1st Player comes on stage and invents movements to a rhythm and tempo of its own choice, counting aloud and stressing the downbeat. 2nd Player must watch and memorize the rhythm and tempo. Allow about 20 seconds before signalling 2nd Player.

1st Player continues as 2nd Player enters and invents a different set of movements, done to the same rhthym and tempo.

Discussion: Did 1st Player keep the same rhythm and tempo all the time? Was 2nd Player able to imitate it? Was there contrast between the Players' movements?

Repeat with different Players, rhythms, tempos.

Problem Q7

RHYTHMIC SOUND EFFECTS

HOME SPACE:
Whole Class

Class in a circle. Set up a finger-snapping beat which is to be picked up one by one around the circle. Keep the tempo going throughout the following changes:

Change to rhythmic clapping with an accented downbeat.

Add vocal sounds: "RING ding-a ding ding, RING ding-a ding ding" ... "Ker-CHEW burp pssss boop" ... "DA diddledy do dip" ..."MMMM click bum bum" and so forth. Keeping the beat going, let volunteers in turn make new nonsense sounds.

Problem Q8

SILENT BEATS

HOME SPACE:
Whole Class

Pre-select music with an obvious 4-beat (usually 4/4 time). You'll use it for (B) below. Establish a 4-beat rhythm by calling the 1st and clapping the 2nd, 3rd, 4th beats. Class joins in.

Repeat but just touch fingertips for "2, 3, 4." Repeat but don't move at all; keep the beat going inside the body or head.

Music. Without coaching, let the children find the beat and clap to it (12 — 15 seconds).

Shift to double time (you may have to demonstrate).

Shift back to straight time; accent beats 1 and 3.

Next: loud clap 1, silent 2 and 3, light clap 4.

Repeat several times as the music plays.

Problem Q9

COMBINING RHYTHMS

THEATRE:
3 Pairs of Players

1st Player walks, counting aloud and clapping a 2-beat rhythm. You may want to reinforce the tempo with a faint drumming (10 or 12 seconds, then stop action).

2nd Player then walks, picking up the same tempo from your drum, but counting and clapping a 3-beat rhythm (10 or 12 seconds, as above).

Now combine the two (15 seconds).

Two new Players, a new rhythm: a 5-count measure worked with a 3-beat, as above.

Two new Players, another new rhythm: a 4-beat, worked with a 5-beat, as above.

Problem Q10

SOUNDS OF THE CITY

HOME SPACE:
Whole Class

Children seated in a circle. In turn, they imitate sounds of the city and its inhabitants. Examples:

shout	**wind**	**church bells**
siren	**laughter**	**car horn**
pigeon	**jet plane**	**dog growl**
whistle	**telephone ring**	**motorbike**
sneeze	**car brake/skid**	**talking**
streetcar bell	**scream**	**helicopter**

Select the best 15 or 18 sounds. Organize the students into three groups and assign a sound to each student. The class is now in the THEATRE mode, divided into Players and Audience. To the Players:

> **Invent a movement to do as you make your sound. It can be part of what *makes* the sound (be a bouncing motorbike rider making the motorbike sound): *descriptive* movement. Or it can be a *reaction* to the sound (make the church bells sound + drop to your knees and pray): *reactive* movement. Or it can be an *interpretive* movement — one that expresses the feeling the sound arouses in you (car honking + an aggressive chest-beating ape).**

Group 1 on stage. Perform in turn, then together.

Repeat with Groups 2 and 3.

Discussion: Which was more interesting: reactive movements, descriptive ones or interpretive ones? Why would you choose to do a descriptive movement with some sounds and a reactive movement with others?

Repeat with the rest of the class if desired. This problem lends itself to continuing development, to composition and to demonstration performance.

The Stage, Travel Paths and Floor Patterns

These exercises will familiarize the students with the terms used to describe stage geography and locomotion in the playing area

Problem R1

THE RITUAL

THEATRE:
Whole Class

Problem 8 in Model Class Plan 1 offers a prelude to the following exercise. The exercise itself is simply a ritual for "framing" performances of other problems.

Have the children sit in a row facing the Dance Space; tell them that they are an *Audience* and in front of them the Dance Space is now going to become the *Stage.*

Place two students DC; they become the *Curtain.* When they move away from each other, off R and off L, the *Curtain* is opening. The *Curtain* is closing when the two students return to DC to hold hands.

Explain that in the real theatre it gets dark in the auditorium just before the show begins; that's a cue for everyone to stop talking and watch for the curtain to open. So when you call out **"house lights going down!"** the **Audience** must become absolutely quiet. When you call **"Curtain!"** the Curtain opens to begin the performance.

At the end of the performance *Curtain* closes again on your cue; *Audience* applauds; *Players* bow.

Problem R2

STAGE CEOGRAPHY

THEATRE:
8 Players

Place 8 Players at the 8 stations around the stage perimeter. The 9th, at C, will be *It* in the game.

UR	UC	UL
R	C	L
DR	DC	DL

Audience

Call out travel commands, eg. "Cross to up left," "Go to down center," etc.

It must run to the specified station, tag the Player there and await the next command.

If *It* hesitates or goes to the wrong spot, the Player at the correct spot becomes *It* and goes to C.

Discussion: Space and travel on the stage are described from the Player's viewpoint, facing the audience. That's why, when you called "Cross right" it looked like *It* crossed to the left.

8 players. Variation on previous game.

As each travel command is called out, players run to the designated area. Last one to get there is out and returns to the audience. Repeat until all but one have been eliminated.

Repeat with another group of 8.

When all have had their chance, have the winners from each group compete as a group in a final play-off.

Problem R3

WHAT ARE TRAVEL PATHS?

DANCE SPACE:
Whole Class

Place the students around the perimeter of the Dance Space. You are in the middle; demonstrate the movements as you describe them.

Discuss travel paths, the imaginary lines along which one moves across the floor. The basic directions are *up, down, across* and *diagonal* (see GLOSSARY, *Stage Geography*). A travel line can go straight in one direction, or curve, or make a pattern such as a *circle, spiral, square, triangle, zigzag, scallops, wavy line (serpentine)* or even a *wandering* irregular path.

Problem R4 (of Set R4-R5)

PRACTICING TRAVEL PATHS

THEATRE:
Trios in turn

1st Player **diagonal line — *scallops* then *square***

2nd Player: **across — *serpentine* then *zigzag***

3rd Player: **spiral — *triangle* then *circle***

Repeat with three more trios.

13th Player: **run on a *serpentine* line**

14th Player: **hop on a *square*d line**

15th Player: **walk on a *curved diagonal* UR to DL.**

229

Problem R5 (of Set R4-R5)

TRANSITIONS

THEATRE:
Individually

The problem is flow smoothly from one kind of locomotor movement to another as one travels along a given path, and to flow smoothly from one travel path to the next. 1st Player illustrates:

> **Move on a *diagonal,* crawling. Jump into a run, then change to a *circular* path. Switch to a walk, then change to a path *straight down.* Switch to a hop and stop.**

Repeat with new Players, who select their own paths and movements.

As above, except that now the locomotor movement changes at the same time as the path changes. This is a bit harder; stress smooth continuous-motion transitions.

Problem R6 (of Set R6-R7)

PATHS, MOVEMENTS, LEVELS

THEATRE:
12 Players

Create 3 groups: 6 Players in Group 1, 4 Players in Group 2 and a pair for Group 3. They will move simultaneously, thus:

Group 1	Group 2	Group 3
Diagonal path	Straight down	Circle
Crawling	Walking waving arms aloft	Skipping holding hands

Level: low   Level: high   Level: medium

Give them their blocking. There are four choices:

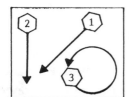 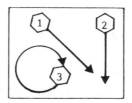 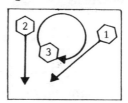 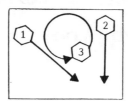

Discussion: Was there good contrast? Would it have been better if different groups had the high, medium and low levels? Would different blocking work better?

Problem R7 (of Set R6-R7)

TRAVEL WITH SECONDARY MOTION AND VOICE

THEATRE:
2 Players

Player 1	**Player 2**
Square path, UC area	Straight path DL to DR
Marching	Jogging
Swinging arms	Flapping elbows
Voice: "1, 2, 3, 4,	Voice: "Add, subtract, add,
1, 2, 3 — " etc	subtract, add — " etc

Discussion: Did both Players seem to be part of the same act — connected? Would it be better if they were blocked differently?

Repeat with another duo; let them choose their own paths, locomotor movements, secondary motions and words.

Problem R8

DESIGNS AND DIAGRAMS

THEATRE: These exercises require paper, pencils or crayons.

Students draw the major travel paths on a sheet of paper (straight up-or-down, straight across, square, circle, wavy, zigzag, diagonal, triangle, and random or wandering) — or as many as they can remember. Those who remember the most paths go onstage; taking turns, they walk and call the name of each path as it is performed. The *Watchers* add to their own drawings any paths they forgot.

Now the *Watchers* take the stage in turn and perform their diagrams, improvising whatever locomotor movements they wish and adding improvised words as in **R 7**, above. As each path is travelled, the Audience shouts the name of the path.

PART 4

Appendices

Appendix A

Fantasy and Imagination

Everyone knows what imagination is, but not everyone has thought about what composes it and what triggers it and how to teach it.

Imagination isn't innate; it's an ordinary habit of the mind. We constantly "imagine" (foresee) a result before we take an action — a process heavily dependent on memory of previous outcomes mediated, perhaps, by new "givens." This is everyday imagination.

Like any other kind of problem-solving, art-making uses everyday imagination constantly, but **creative imagination**, which we also call **fantasy**, involves departing from the everyday, from the familiar, and mentally inventing or combining or juxtaposing *unfamiliar* things and imaging extraordinary processes.

This happens involuntarily in dreams, of course (which themselves can be a source of art-making). Here, however, we are interested in helping wide-awake children enter into and use fantasy in art-making — communicating in poetry rather than prose, dealing in feelings rather than abstractions.

Here is one practical way to think about creative imagination. It involves ...

Acts of association

Verbally: similes and metaphors. "That far-off clump of trees looks like a bunch of broccoli." "The moon is drowning in the sea." Is there anyone who hasn't seen animal shapes, castles, mountain ranges in the clouds? (Answer: maybe, until someone showed the child how to look). Free association exercises (letting a word, sound or image evoke another word or image) are a very basic way of cultivating the imagination. These can be developed as a string of associations: teakettle > steam locomotive > express train > roller coaster. Free association exercises lend themselves to classroom practice.

Transformations

Changes in size or scale. In one of Robert Louis Stevenson's poems the child watches leaves floating in the brook and sees them as ships sailing toward the sea and beyond to strange lands. Or the swimmer, floating face down along the rock-face, looks at the sandy bottom ten feet down and imagines coral cliffs rising from a vast yellow plain far below. The seaweed seems mysterious — a tropical jungle, the tiny fish some sort of exotic aircraft maneuvering above it.

There are transformations of other kinds: changes of kind, of tempo, of quality, sometimes taking place as mental cinema. This happens frequently in dreams. The great acting teacher Michael Chekhov recommends an exercise with eyes closed: visualize a young man; fix on the image with maximum concentration, watch him gradually grow old until he's bald, bent, toothless and lame ... and gradually restore him again — or let him die peacefully and give him a fantastic funeral.

Anomalies

Incongruous combinations of features or elements. Mythology is rich with anomalies: Pegasus (the winged horse), unicorns, mermaids, centaurs, the Aztec Plumed Serpent, animals with human voices (the Serpent in the Garden of Eden spoke to Eve), spirits who inhabit trees, waters, valleys, mountains and the sky. A famous episode in the bygone TV show, *Candid Camera*, involved a talking mailbox whose contents begged passersby to "please help me get out of here".

Empathy

This may be the commonest kind of imagination — feeling one's way into the feelings of another. It comes naturally to children. In art, it is the primary fantasy-tool of the actor.

Appendix B

Music

Music has biological dimensions; its rhythms are like those of the heart, of breathing, of many motor activities ... and of course, mysteriously, music can evoke kinetic impulses that answer music's own rhythms: we want to dance, "conduct," beat time with clapping hands, nodding heads and tapping toes.

Equally mysterious is music's way of arousing feeling. But maybe not so mysterious at that — after all, isn't music simply speaking in code about the human condition? The human voice's inflections, accents and intonations have all been borrowed by music and have the same emotional values as speech — purified and intensified. All the descriptive notations in a musical score can apply equally to human speech: forte, piano, sostenuto, staccato, scherzo, andante and the rest.

Thus music projects human images, sentiments, memories, moods, impulses, actions. It talks to us in sweet code about ourselves. But what makes music music is that it arouses us to sense qualities of existence not ordinarily present in our consciousness.

Listen to lots of music. Make notes of pieces and passages whose qualities (tempo, mood, energy level) may stimulate children in your classroom. Remember, rhythm is mankind's great organizer of gross motor activity, while melody and phrasing evoke the *qualities* of movement.

Because of its suggestive nature, music is especially useful with younger age groups, who are venturing into body awareness, motor control and qualities of movement.

Sensitize the children to the affective qualities of music by asking them how the music makes them feel; build on their responses verbally with suggestive imagery.

Teach the children how to hear a musical phrase: play a fragment with only one, two or three instrumental voices, spot the beginning and with your own gesture lead through to the end of the phrase. Repeating the music, let the children improvise movement to match the phrase.

Stay away from richly orchestrated music (the big symphonies) ... altho there may be passages in almost any music that you'll want to excerpt.

Put whatever you're going to use on a class tape. It's almost impossible to keep class momentum up to speed if you're changing records and hunting for the groove.

CLASS WORK MUSIC BANK

This is a "starter" listing. Any number of pieces can equally well serve. Use material *you* enjoy.

SELECTIONS BASED ON MOOD QUALITY

Agitated: Charles Ives, *Piano Sonata No. 1*
Carefree: Horace Silver Quintet, *Song for my Father*
Frantic: Thea Musgrave, *Composers at the Piano*, Learner Driver
Frolicky: Mark Nelson, *Fiddle Tunes for Dulcimer*, Cherokee Shuffle, band 3
Fun: Dag Achatz, piano, *For Children*, (Debussy) Golliwog's Cakewalk
Joy: Dag Achatz, piano, *For Children*, (Schumann) Kinderzenen Opus 15
Languorous (slow, dreamy): Ben Webster, *Over the Rainbow*
     Miles Davis, in Rodrigo's *Concerto de Aranjuez*
Lively: Los Calchakis, *La Flute Indienne*, Pescadores

Lyrical: Dag Achatz, piano, *For Children,* (Beethoven) *Fur Elise*

Melancholy: Jerome Moross, *Sonatina for Contrabass and Piano*

Pensive: Narciso Yepes, in Rodrigo's *Concierto de Aranjuez,* band 2

Plaintive: Daglash & Larsen, *Banish Misfortune*

Playful: Dag Achatz, piano, *For Children* band 10 (Bartok)

Restless: Kurt Weill, *Kleine Dreigroschenmusik fur Blas-orchester* side 1 cut 2

Sad: Kabalevsky *A Little Song Opus 27 Book 1*

Serene: Bach, *Jesu, Joy of Man's Desiring*

Spooky: Stockhausen, *Electronic Study I* side 1 band 2

Tensions: Columbia, *2001 Space Odyssey;*

  The Gifted Ones (Basie, Brown, Gillespie, Roker), *Saint James Infirmary* side 2

Tentative and timid: Thea Musgrave, *Composers at the Piano,* Excursions

SOME ETHNIC AND FOLK SELECTIONS

Grant Johannesen, pianist: *Brazilian Preludes* 20 Ponteios

Manos Hadjidakis: *April 45 Lilacs Out of the Dead Land*

(Classic Editions): *Rumanian Folk Dance*

(Folkways Records): *Tribal Music of Australia*

(Folkways Records): *Yoruba Elewe - Bata Drums & Dance*

(Saydisc Records): Jing Ying Soloists: *Like Waves Against the Sand*

(Lyrichord Records): *Chinese Opera and Folk Themes*

(Folkways Records): *Folk Music of Hungary*

(Philips Records): *Les Troubadours Missa Luba*

(Folkways Records): *Africa South of the Sahara*

(Reprise Record): Miriam Makeba *Pata Pata*

(Columbia Records): *The Story of the Blues*

(Vanguard Records): *Mississippi John Hurt Today*

(Yazoo Records): *The Young Big Bill Boonzy*

(Yazoo Records): *Blind Willie McTell - Early Years*

(Chess Records): *Howlin' Wolf Evil*

(Monitor Records): inti-illimani -2 *Haeia la Libertad*

(Pablo Records): Joe Pass & Paulinho de Costa *Tudo Bem*

(Stan Getz - Luiz Bonfa): *Jazz Samba Encore*

(Sine Qua Non Records): *An Anthology of Folk Music*

(Folkways Records): Woody Guthrie *Why, oh Why?*

(Folkways Records): Pete Seeger *Animal Folksongs*

(Columbia Records): *World Library of Folk and Primitive Music*

(S A R Productions): *38 Favorite American Folksongs*

A FEW CLASSIC JAZZ FAVORITES

(Nonesuch Records): Scott Joplin, *Piano Rags*

(Columbia Records): *Smithsonian Collection of Classic Jazz*

(Stereo Records): *Louis Armstrong's Greatest Hits*

(RCA Records): *Benny Goodman ,* 3-record set
    History of Jazz Piano

CLASSICAL MUSIC FOR CHILDREN

J. S. Bach: *Two and Three Part Inventions and Sinfonias,* Glen Gould, piano,
    Columbia
    Switched-on Bach, Trans-Electronic Music with Walter Carlos & Benj.
    Folkman, Columbia

Bartok: *Microcosm / Selections,* Book I, II, III, IV, V, VI Dagmar Baloghova, piano, Columbia. *Three Studies / Out of Doors Suite,* Noel Lee, piano, Nonesuch

Beethoven: *Moonlight & Appassionata Sonatas / Pathetique,* Glenn Gould, Columbia

Chopin: *The Complete Mazurkas,* Vol II Nos 22 - 38, Alexander Brailowsky, piano, Columbia

The Chopin Waltzes, Dinu Lipatti, piano, Odyssey

Sonata No 3 in B Minor, Dinu Lipatti, piano, EMI

Copland: *Piano Sonata and Other Works,* Orion

Rodeo and Billy the Kid, Columbia

Appalachian Spring / El Salon Mexico, Columbia

Debussy: *Fifteen Piano Pieces,* Walter Gieseking, piano, Angle

Images / Pour Le Piano / Estampes, Walter Gieseking, piano, Angle

Prelude a L'Apres Midi D'un Faune, Deca

Kabalevsky: *Twenty-four Preludes for Piano,* Nadia Reisenberg, piano, Westminster

MacDowell: *Woodland Sketches Op. 51 / Sea Pieces Op. 55 /Fireside Tales Op. 61 and 62,* Columbia

Moross: *Sonatinas For Divers Instruments,* Desto

Orff and Keetman: *Musica Poetica Vol 1-5 and 6-10,* Harmonia Mundi

Poulenc: *Sonata For Clarinet and Piano / Sonata For Oboe and Piano,* Fevrier, piano / Boutard, clarinet / Pierlot, oboe. Nonesuch

Prokofiev: *Music For Children, Op. 65,* Gresko, piano, London

Ravel: *Quartet in F Major / Introduction and Allegro For Flute, Clarinet and String Quartet,* Melos Ensemble of London, Angle

Satie:: *The Velvet Gentleman,* Camarata Contemporary Chamber Group Deca

Shostakovich: *Six Children's Pieces,* Pressler, piano, M-G-M

Ballet Suites Nos. 1,2,3, Bolshoi Theatre Orchestra, Melodiya

Vivaldi: *The Four Seasons,* Philips

EDUCATIONAL SELECTIONS

Phoebe James: *Creative Rhythms For Children*

Ella Jenkins: *Adventures In Rhythms/Rhythms In Childhood*

Betty King: *Modern Dance - Music For Composition*

Sara Malament, pianist: *Improvisations For Modern Dance*

Cameron McCosh: *Rhythms - Modern Dance*

Howard Mitchell: *Adventures In Music - A New Record Libary For Elementary Schools*

Recording Society: *Marches of All Nations - The Family Library of Beautiful Listening*

Recording Society: *Treasury Of Waltzes - The Family Library of Beautiful Listening*

The Artist-Teacher Partnership

NOTES FOR THE ARTIST WORKING IN A SCHOOL SETTING

Begin with a Conference

The classroom teacher and you are colleagues sharing the same general goal. You are developing the children in two quite different ways — you, the artist, are cultivating imagination, creativity, expressiveness, self-empowerment; the teacher's mandate is to impart knowledge and the skills required to use it, such as writing. Altho all this is integrated within the child's consciousness, your methods and the teacher's obviously require different curriculums and class plans.

Who does what?

Discuss and establish your complementary functions. There are mundane matters: the issues of responsibility for the working area, for dealing with the occasional disruptive situation, the demands of special events. But the important thing is to tell the teacher your objectives for the year. Learn what the teacher's objectives are — not only subject matter but the primary needs of the class. You probably have more flexibility than the teacher; can you adapt your classroom problems to relate to the children's special needs?

Let's say it's an ESL class. Why not produce a performance based on poems? The homeroom teacher can discuss the poems in class — content, word-meanings, imagery — and have the children memorize the verses. When you have made your staging concept, probably involving different "voices," share it with the teacher, who then can break down the memorizing to fit the patterns you've established.

But perhaps the teacher now wants you to orient toward a certain subject matter. Discuss it — can you develop a theme into which you can fit your class plans, so that your classes echo or play off what the children are learning in school? Some subject matter lends itself to artistic expression — some doesn't. With imagination on both sides a fruitful partnership can develop.

Scene and Two Fables

BARNYARD

A Sample Classroom Scene

This little scene is an extension of the problems in animal modeling detailed in the *Class Work Bank* (Chap. 10). It shouldn't be attempted until the class has spent a good deal of time on problems A2 through A5. Remember, the name of the game is not mimicry. It is to select a body part whose movement conveys the essential characteristic of the animal; it is an exercise in movement quality.

Each character in this scene must have an objective, an obstacle and a sense of the environment. Leave the rest up to the children.

Afternoon: Hot. Quiet. A sense of endless time.

Onstage: Pig, Snake, Baby Chick, Rooster.

Offstage: Farmer.

Beginning: Pig and Snake are dozing. Baby Chick is eating, pecking the ground. Rooster is grooming himself.

Middle: Farmer comes into the barnyard, tired. Stretches out, swats a couple of flies, falls asleep.

Pig rouses up, goes over to wallow in the mud. Snake also rouses and begins to slide along, sneaking up on Baby Chick.

As Snake approaches, Baby Chick hops up and over the wallowing Pig and then begins to pick off ticks.

Rooster see Snake, puffs up, flaps, paws dirt, crows.

Snake changes course; goes and coils up on Farmer's belly.

Farmer wakes up, sees Snake, utters a loud yell and rushes off. Snake slithers away.

Baby Chick and Pig do a little run after the vanishing Snake, while Rooster crows and dances.

End: Activity dies down. One by one they resume their original positions and activities. Once again, all is quiet.

DISCOVERY ISLAND

The Scenario for a Fable

Discovery Island requires the talents of a mask-maker and the creation of a master tape with narration and music.

Characters: Survivors, Grey Magician, 2 Assistants who function as kabuki propmen. Masks: Grey Magician, Fury, Fear, 2 Warriors, 3 Smiling masks.

Setting: The only basic requirement is a prop table UC on which rest short lengths of rope and masks when not in use.

Narration	Action
There is a storm at sea. A ship is lost. Survivors row toward land ... and land.	Tape narration (recommended), or a live Narrator sets the stage and introduces the Survivors. They bow to the audience. They take their lifeboat positions and row wearily until their boat capsizes in the surf. Flung out, they wade ashore, collapse and rest.
Grey Magician appears with his Assistants, welcomes the castaways, tells them this beautiful bountiful land is theirs, suggests that they mark off gardens for food.	Narrator introduces the Grey Magician and Assistants. They bow deeply. Stylized gesture as the Narrator speaks for the Grey Magician.
	Assistants distribute lengths of rope. The Survivors with their boundary ropes do a simple ceremonial dance of joy as they mark off their gardens.
But two fall into a dispute over one of the garden boundaries.	Magician and Assistants have retired to the prop table. With backs to audience all three change masks. Magician is now Fury. The prop men are now Warriors.

They challenge and threaten.	Meantime DC the quarrelers are doing a dance of conflict. When one finally shoves or strikes the other, the three upstage figures wheel around and Fury the War God rules.
War is imminent.	The Warriors organize the Players into two armies. Maneuvers and war games now begin. Warriors return to the prop table; one gets the Fear mask while the other takes the Fury mask from the player who's wearing it.
War begins. Side Alpha attacks.	Warriors put the Fury mask on the Alpha leader and the Fear mask on the head of the Omegas. In choreographed battle the Alphas attack, the Omegas retreat.
But the tide turns.	Warriors switch the Fear and Fury masks and the Alpha/Omega choreography is reversed. There is a crescendo. The Fear and Fury masks can be removed, passed around wildly, thrust up like rearing snakes. But the energy fades.
War weariness sets in. The troops refuse to fight.	The Grey Magician player and the Warriors are at the prop table, facing up, changing into the 3 Smiling masks and picking up 3 ceremonial staffs. Coming to UC, they strike the ground thrice with their staffs.

The troops begin to fraternize. The war is over.	The troops divide to reveal them. The prop men recover the Fury and Fear masks from the troops, place them back on the prop table. They return with the Grey Magician mask. The Survivors are doing a dance of shared fatigue and sorrow.
Reconciliation and reconstruction begin.	The Grey Magician now dons his own mask; his assistants are still Smiling.
Grey magician now proposes, instead of separate gardens, a single big garden, worked together.	Again, it's the Narrator's voice, with a simple flowing gesture or two by the player.
	Now a reprise of the original dance of pleasure on the island, and of harmonious planting and growing. Grey Magician and Assistants put aside their masks and join in.
But nothing is ever completely assured...	One player steals back to the prop table, tries on the Fury mask and tries a warlike pose. The others rush up, remove the mask .... and all, holding hands, come down for the bow.

THE OUTSIDER

A Scenario

The Outsider is stylized; natural movement should be enlarged and its quality somewhat heightened (e.g. energy made more energetic, languor more languorous). This has the effect of communicating generalizations or implicit meanings rather than literal description. The students are choruses or teams. Individualizing the Outsider and Anna must be minimal: they represent, respectively, loneliness and friendliness and not specific people. The whole piece is a metaphor, not a documentary. Each of the little scenes below is extended choreographically, and some choreographic experience is necessary if the piece is to be done as written.

Characters: Young school children, teacher (on tape)

Setting: A school — at first in the classroom, indicated only by chairs, then the schoolyard — a bare stage.

School teacher is summoned away temporarily and leaves Anna to lead in the lesson. As the door closes, bedlam begins. It ends only when Teacher's voice offstage restores order.

Anna leads the class in a sing-song exercise. Talk begins about the "new kid," becoming a game of out-doing one another in horrid one-line descriptions. Recess is announced.

The Outsider, a small girl, is alone in the playground. Singing a little song of loneliness, she dances sadly, interrupted by the children pouring out into the yard for recess. She drops to the ground in a ball UL (or UR) as three different games begin. One of the game-groups is led by Anna.

Anna and her group encounter the Outsider, draw her in and take her toward the others for acceptance. But first one then others in turn begin to tease with cruel insults. They exit in formation, except for one who turns to watch Anna's group, which now begins a dance of friendship and support for the Outsider. The watcher now comes to join them; another child re-enters and watches.

All go off as friends as the dance ends.

All come on holding hands for the bow

A Few Good Books

Barlin. *The Art of Learning Through Movement.* Ward Ritchie Press 1971

Dimondstein. *Children Dance in the classroom.* Macmillan 1971

Dorian. *Ethnic Stories for Children to Dance.* BBB Associates 1978

Flinchum. *Motor Development in Early Childhood.* C. V. Mosby Co. 1975

Frostig and Maslow. *Learning Problems in the Classroom.* Tollman Hall

Humphrey. *The Art of Making Dances.* Grove Press 1959

Kreitler and Kreitler. *Psychology of the Arts.* Duke University Press

Mettler. *Materials of Dance.* Mettler Studios, 3131 N. Cherry Av., Tuscon, AR
  1960 rev 1979
  Group Dance Improvisations. Mettler Studios 1975

Murray. *Dance in Elementary Education.* Harper-Row 1963

Spolin. *Theatre Games for the Classroom.* Northwestern University Press 1986

Johnstone. *Impro (Improvisation and the Theatre).* Theatre Arts Book 1984

Stanislavski. *Building a Character.* Theatre Arts Book 1976

Boleslavsky. *Acting.* Dennis Dobson LTD London 1949

The Mechanics of Learning

IN THE BEGINNING IS THE BODY

It has been wisely noted that a child's body is the one ever-present feature of its environment. To control it is the infant animal's first task. Its form and characteristics are the visible components of self — the first inspiration for a self-image. It is the body's ability to move that enables learning to take place. Motor activity is indispensable to cognitive development.

Ultimately self-image is a totalized sum of perceived attributes. In the most formative years, however, the child's body and rapidly-increasing physical skills are the most salient influences (along with parental attitudes) on self-image. Indeed throughout life one's self-image is affected by various properties of the body, including notably its motor skills. But although the body's role in self-image may diminish as one matures, the importance of cognitive development increases; general competence comes to depend more heavily on intellectual skills.

Cognition is an extraordinarily complex process involving intricate neural activities in the brain, but it can be crudely generalized as *perceptual motor activity* — motor activity triggered by perception. Structural psychologists use a computer model diagram to describe the process:

$$\rightarrow \text{INPUT} \rightarrow \text{INTEGRATION} \rightarrow \text{MOTOR RESPONSE}$$
$$\longleftarrow \text{feedback} \leftarrow \text{OUTCOME} \leftarrow$$

Input: There is a sensory stimulus impinging on the vision, hearing, touch, taste, smell ... a perception of some kind.

Integration: To continue the computer analogy, the brain seeks to match the incoming datum to its coded-and-stored information bank (the memory, conscious or subconscious). Through logic-type operations a motor response (a response in the form of muscle motion) is initiated.   Will it be appropriate? That depends on what has been previously learned from comparable stimuli.

Motor Response: This may a fine motor movement, such as focusing the eyes, activating the vocal chords, lacing a shoe ... or a gross motor reaction like reaching, turning, dodging, sitting, walking. In early stages of growth this motor response is itself an act of testing to learn the aptness of the action.

Feedback: The outcome of the response is sped back to the brain, thus becoming input and becoming a new datum in the memory bank, validating or modifying or invalidating previously stored data.

This cycle comprises the basic connection between physical movement and cognitive development.

Cognitive development naturally occurs in proportion to the frequency, variety and potency of inputs. Driven by biological imperatives, happily normal young children are eager experimenters — they actively seek "inputs." Here there are two cardinal points for teachers:

> 1. Learning and thinking skills are fostered by a wide range of alternatives for thought and action.

> 2. Learning and thinking are especially fostered by the unusual, the unexpected, the incongruous.

Repetition and rote may have uses for memorizing data or motor operations, but they contribute little to cognitive ability — to the ability to discriminate, conceptualize, envision a spread of alternatives, analyze and choose among them (all those faculties essential to competent or creative problem-solving).

Individuals tends to develop different cognitive styles of problem-solving. Two of the commonest in art-making are the analytic style and the synthesizing style. The analytic art-maker begins by identifying the salient attribute(s) of the subject or problem at hand. In the synthesizing style, a mental connection is made between things, or between a thing and a concept, or between two concepts.

Example from classroom art-making:

The given problem: to communicate with body movement the concept of roundness. *Solution:* the young student extends her left arm at a downward angle. With her right hand she places an imaginary object on her left shoulder and releases it. Swiftly her eyes track it down and off the end, to the floor and back up in a bounce and "catches" it — obviously a ball.

Now one of the salient characteristics of roundness is its rollability. So choosing to pantomime something rolling was an analytic act. Of course a hoop can roll, or a cylinder or a plate, although they are round in only one plane. But a sphere is *round* round — nothing is rounder than a ball. So a connection was made among roundness and rolling and bouncing, and the synthesis communicated a ball, the very symbol and essence of roundness.

Life is governed by causality; cause and effect are expressed as rules. The growing learning child acquires rules for various specific areas — the physical world , the world of interpersonal relationships, of skill acquisition, of managing emotion ... rules, in short, for how things and people function and *how they can be operated on.* Clearly the more sets of rules the child understands and the more it masters the functions of both imagination and logic in the problem-solving process, the greater the child's competence. Moreover there is a transfer or cross-over factor in competence; competence in one field facilitates competence in others — simply because certain basic cognitive processes apply to most problems. Hence the emphasis in this book on a "basic problem-solving method" (cf. *Introduction*).

One of the most important set of rules comes under the heading: *Socialization.* Children must discover the operative value systems, hierarchical roles, partnership roles and appropriate modes of human intercourse. Group play is, of course, a prime agency for socialization — not only in the very young, where its role is pivotal, but on into adult life as well. And *play is the progenitor of art,* both individual and collective. Art-making in group settings, the subject of this volume, is thus another school for socialization. It is weighted with affirmative values, foremost of which is learning to fulfill the roles of both Player and Watcher, giver and receiver, and how to be both commender and critic.

Appendix G

Using Multi-cultural Resources

In communities in which there are ethnic dancers, a school can enlist such a performer for a "residency" of 15 to 30 once-a-week classes. In concert with geography and social studies, involvement with ethnic dance is an admirable way to explore the cultural similarities and differences within the human family. It is inviting to children because it's vivid; it awakens physical empathy; it nourishes new perceptions; and it tends to internalize that new knowledge thru creative involvement. Above all it helps dissolve conscious and subconscious ethnic alienations.

The dancer, brought into the classroom, recounts the legends, the beliefs, the many human activities from which the dances derive. The children then learn actual dances.

Two things now have happened. The parochialism of the dominant culture begins to dissolve into a more world-oriented view — and a strong positive message comes to children from the culture represented by the artist: the artist has become a role model, an affirmation of ethnic worth.

Maximizing the experience requires that there be a collaboration between the classroom teacher and the guest artist — enhanced by maps, videos, pictorial and written matter. Later, as the children master the choreography they've been rehearsing, they should be challenged to invent body movements and rhythms derived from their contemporary life — of play, work, family life — and make brief little dances (solo or group) of their own.

To make the whole experience most rewarding, it should culminate in a public showing — a school assembly, a neighborhood event or any other occasion that suggests itself.

Glossary

A

ABA, ABCBD, etc   Code for the arrangement or pattern of formal elements in a composition. Used in dance, **ABA** means that the thematic sequence **A** reappears after an intermediate sequence **B** (altho **A** is usually condensed its second time around). In poetry, the code refers to the rhyme scheme.

Action   See *Playing an Action,* below.

Accent   Used as a verb: to make prominent a specific, sound, movement, rhythmic beat or spot within a pattern. As a noun: such spots.

Ad lib   To suit yourself; to improvise. An extemporaneous line or speech.

Adjustment   In acting: the imagined circumstances in which the Player plays an action. See Givens.

Affect   Used as a noun: feeling, emotion.

Attitude   Referring to the body: expressive posture or body shape.

B

Balance   In composition: the arrangement of equivalent forms, masses, colors, musical patterns on either side of an imagined central point. When the two sides flanking the central point mirror each other the balance is *symmetrical.* When they are unalike but demand equal attention it is called *occult* or *asymmetrical* balance.

Beat	1. A unit of time. In music it's the unit that establishes the time pattern (4/4 time = 4 beats in a measure). Repetitive accenting of a certain beat (usually the downbeat) creates a rhythm.
	2. In timing any stage action: one second, a count of "a thousand and one" said fairly fast.
	3. In acting: a mini-scene or period in which the action is not modified by introducing any new element.
Blocking	To establish the positions of players and the pattern of their large movements on stage.
B-M-E	In composition: beginning, middle and end. The beginning establishes a situation. The middle introduces something new and the resulting actions. The end contains some kind of resolution, sometimes containing elements or echoes of the beginning. (See ABA).

C

C	Abbreviation for Center Stage (see Stage Geography).
Choreography	See *Blocking,* and add the design of expressive motion, tempo, timing, rhythm, dynamics; total dance composition.
Cognitive	Pertaining to mental functions; perceiving and thinking.
Crescendo	An increase or swelling of sound.

D

DC, DL, DR	Downstage center, down left, down right (see Stage Geography).

Demo's   Class demonstrations.

Diminuendo   Diminishment of sound; opposite of crescendo.

Downstage   Toward the audience.

Dynamics   The arousing of energy and the subsequent harnessing, focussing, and modulating of that energy.

E

Empathy   Identifying with another being; experiencing in the imagination what that other being is experiencing.

ESL   English as a Second Language: a category of students whose families use a language other than English.

F

Facings   The direction in which the Player on stage is facing relative to the audience: full front; 1/4; side or profile; 3/4; full back or straight up.

G

Givens   In acting: all the elements (both subjective and external) present when an action is to be played. Taken all together they comprise the "Situation. "

H

House   In theatre terms, 1) the auditorium facing the stage, or 2), at a performance, the audience in the auditorium.

I

Improv   In acting: improvisation.

J

Justify   In acting: to imagine the Givens that enable one to play an action with artistic truthfulness, belief.

K

Kabuki prop men In the Japanese Kabuki theatre, properties are manipulated or handed to performers in full view of the audience by prop men dressed in black, symbolizing invisibility.

Kinesthetic   More properly, kinesthesia. The sensation of body movement, of energy flow activating the muscles.

Kinetic   The energy involved in movement. Cf. Potential energy.

L

Locomotor   Traveling movement: walk, run, skip, gallop, etc.

M

Meter   The succession of regularly-spaced stressed notes (in music) or syllables (in poetry). Same as the time signature in music, e.g. 3/4 time (in verse: dactylic meter).

O

Objective   Acting: that which the character is after in a given situation. Also used for long term aims.

Obstacle   Acting: the major impediment to achieving an objective. Minor impediments can be classed as givens.

P

Phrasing   The pattern of energy release and expression, the rises and falls of intensity and tempo in a movement (or musical or vocal) sequence.

Playing an action   In acting: striving with total concentration to achieve an immediate objective.

Potential energy   Stored energy available to be released in motion; in acting — contained or pent-up energy, ready for release.

Props   "Properties." Hand props are objects handled by the Players; stage props are items of furniture or decor.

R

Reprise In music, a return to and repetition of the original theme after an intervening section.

Rest In music, a brief silence of a measured duration which does not disturb the tempo or rhythm.

Rhythm A more or less regular pattern of recurring sound or movement. May be no more than the meter (time signature), but may also refer to manipulations *within* the meter (e.g. syncopation) or to larger patterns of stressed notes.

S

Scenario Story outline, sequence of action and events.

Stage geography

UR	UC	UL	**Upstage Right, Up Center, Up Left**
RC	C	LC	**Right Center, Center, Left Center**
DR	DC	DL	**Down Right, Down Center, Down Left**
	AUDIENCE		These terms are named from the Player's viewpoint facing the house.

Movement from point to point is "crossing" (e.g. "Cross up left" ... Written: XUL).

T

Theatre mode   We use this term to connote the performance situation in the classroom, in which there is a communication/response exchange between Players and Watchers.

U

Upstage   Away from the audience.

X

X   Written symbol for "cross," i.e. to move from one part of the stage to another.